The Vict

M A C Horne FCILT

Capital Transport

First published 2004

ISBN 185414 281 X

Published in association with London's Transport Museum
by Capital Transport Publishing, P.O. Box 250, Harrow, Middlesex

Printed by CS Graphics, Singapore

CONTENTS

cut travel time

victoria line

all about the Victoria Line
- times
- fares from August 1970
- **how to use the automatic gates**

This design was used for Victoria Line publicity from the time of its opening in 1968, the initial letter of the line being formed by the open scissors.
LT Museum

Introduction and Background

The Victoria Line is so far the only complete underground railway line to be built across central London since the Edwardian era, although there have been extensions to many other lines during the last hundred years or so. In this chapter the more distant history of the Victoria Line is in those schemes based on railways linking Finsbury Park with Victoria, and Victoria with south London.

Although post-war Britain was the stage upon which the Victoria Line developments were enacted, the scene was really set in the pre-war world of 1933. During the course of that year the London Passenger Transport Board (LPTB) was formed and from 1st July the LPTB had the responsibility of running all the Underground lines, bus and tramway services in a huge area in and around London.

The LPTB inherited both a deep-level system of tube railways, and a largely separate network of shallow tunnel and open-air railways. The 'surface' system consisted of the substantially Victorian origin Circle, District and Metropolitan Lines, largely bordering or operating outside the central area. The tube lines were more recent (but still Victorian and Edwardian) and had been built as relatively short, high capacity, frequent-interval lines which mainly criss-crossed central London. After the First World War the emphasis of development was to utilise the surplus capacity of the increasingly efficient tubes by projecting them outwards into the suburbs-to-be, generating new traffic as they went. The desire for building new (and expensive) central London tubes thus diminished.

This general trend continued until the Second World War. Afterwards the 'Green Belt' philosophy stopped London's outward expansion and there were serious expenditure and materials restrictions followed by an explosion in car ownership, all of which took the impetus away for further significant transport development in the outer areas. But the demand for in-town services did continue to rise, fuelled by central London office development, increasing road congestion and the growth of longer-distance commuting on the main line railways. Inevitably this began to place some of the central area stations under considerable pressure – the time was ripe for considering once more the building of new tube lines across central London. A feature of the 1933 arrangements was that both the Board and the main line railways were party to a statutory revenue-pooling scheme for local passenger services provided within the London Area. The Pool was administered by a Standing Joint Committee of the LPTB and the railway companies, though the former was very much the more influential partner. The revenue pool meant that the jealousies and rivalries between the transport operators of the 1920s were suppressed, and that co-operation (increasing the total revenue of the Pool) benefited all the partners. Within months of the formation of the LPTB a large-scale programme of new investment was being developed which became the 1935–40 New Works Programme. A result of this administrative arrangement was that the new works, in addition to extending several tube lines, involved the electrification of some main line branches with Underground trains taking over the passenger services.

In 1936 an LPTB team visited New York where they were much taken with that city's rapid transit system where railway lines carrying the 'all stations' services were often duplicated by 'express' lines with occasional facilities for interchange between the two. This both increased carrying capacity and made for a quicker and more attractive journey to and from the outer areas. This left a definite mark in LPTB thinking.

At about the same time it began to be accepted that despite modernisation work, London's existing central area lines would be placed under severe pressure by all the additional traffic from the proposed outer London extensions. In the light of the New York visit 'express' tubes were suggested, one paralleling the Central Line between Liverpool Street and Marble Arch, and another paralleling the Northern Line between Archway and Tottenham Court Road. Connections would be made to the existing tracks at each end. Another proposal was for a new express tube from Victoria via Bond Street and Baker Street to Finchley Road and the Metropolitan Line, with interconnections with the Bakerloo Line at Baker Street.

In the following year, 1937, the LPTB's General Manager (Railways) put forward tentative proposals for a further programme of works, to be built between 1940 and 1950. The man concerned was John Pattinson Thomas, who had been a major influence in the drafting of the 1935–40 New Works Programme. He adopted a consistent approach, and again planned to incorporate several branch lines of the London & North Eastern Railway (LNER) into the Underground. Thomas envisaged electrification of the Palace Gates, Enfield Town and Chingford branches to London Transport standards and plugging them into a new tube railway heading towards Finsbury Park (a similar process was then taking place with the 1935–40 Central Line eastern extensions to Hainault and Ongar). From this point it was thought that part of the service could operate to the City via the existing Northern City tube, on which there was spare capacity beyond that required for the proposed new Northern Line services to Alexandra Palace and High Barnet. The balance of the service would continue due south-west in a new express tube towards Victoria via the West End.

The express tube was in essence the proposed Archway to Tottenham Court Road line, diverted at the northern end to Finsbury Park and extended at the southern end. Intermediate stations were speculatively suggested at Camden Town, Tottenham Court Road and Piccadilly Circus. The objective of this alignment was to divert a proportion of existing traffic away from two of the busiest sections of the Underground, on the Piccadilly and Northern Lines. The line would also divert passengers from Liverpool Street and the Central Line, heavily used in the central area and still deemed to need its own 'relief' express tube once its eastern extensions opened.

Another component of Thomas's plan was a revival of an old idea – a tube railway from Cricklewood to Victoria via the Edgware Road, Marble Arch and Hyde Park Corner (which effectively superseded the Victoria–Baker Street 1936 scheme). This time a large-diameter tube was contemplated, with a view to connecting with the St Pancras main line.

These schemes were highly speculative but are the first indications of the general transport corridors along which it was felt necessary to improve services by means of completely new construction. During subsequent government discussions in mid-1938 the proposals were illustrated to show the nature of the developments required. These were still broadly similar to Thomas's 1937 proposals and included the Finsbury Park to Victoria tube, although the northern termini were now unspecified. The Chingford and Edmonton branches were listed separately among other lines to be electrified (by the LNER), and no specific link with the new tube was indicated.

The government's support was vital, and the relevant Assistant Secretary proved very supportive in putting forward the Board's proposals to his Minister. This set out a case for further expenditure of the order of £50–£60million on London's transport facilities, a programme at least as large (at 1940s prices) as the 1935–40 New Works. However, the financial background against which the new proposals were considered was not favourable. The cost of the 1935–40 programme had been underestimated and various modifications, and inflation, had taken their toll. The Board had insufficient spare cash to meet the additional costs and the LNER was already in serious financial difficulty. Some aspects of the programme were only retained because of contractual or legal obligations, and critical eyes continued to look at areas where substantial economies could be made. This was hardly the best position from which to embark on building new railways. In those days cash support for new construction was not available for railway purposes, only privileged borrowing that attracted interest and would ultimately need repayment.

It was not until 7th January 1939 that the Standing Joint Committee of the LPTB and main line companies called for a report, 'offering a preliminary view of requirements for new transport facilities for London in the following ten years', in other words ideas for another 'New Works' programme. The report was signed on 31st August, three days before war against Germany was declared, and hardly any longer a priority. Nevertheless it does indicate a further development of ideas.

The 1939 plan reviewed the existing sections of overcrowded railway but was now markedly unenthusiastic about mere duplication of railway lines (except at the south end of the Northern Line) on the grounds that the duplicate lines would only be of value during the peak hours. It was now felt that in order to justify relief facilities new railways would also have to serve new areas in order to build up a base traffic of their own. Two major railway schemes were included. Electrification of the Midland and the High Wycombe–Marylebone main lines was one such scheme, with trains from each projected via a new tube through the West End to Victoria (clearly superseding the 'Cricklewood' tube proposal of 1937).

The Victoria to Finsbury Park proposal was also developed further. Stage 1 envisaged duplicating the Northern Line between Morden and Clapham Common, but on a shorter alignment. From Clapham Common a new line would then run towards a temporary terminus at Victoria. With the Northern Line trains running express through the new tube from Morden to Clapham Common, calling only at Tooting Broadway, and the existing 'all stations' service from Morden diverging from the old route at Clapham Common and running express to Victoria, passengers could interchange as necessary at Clapham Common. The combination of both lines would significantly speed up the journey time from the outer reaches.

Stage 2 of the new line was similar in principle to the earlier Victoria–Finsbury Park proposal but on a slightly different route via Green Park, Bond Street, Great Portland Street, thence to Camden Town and express to Finsbury Park. This reflected a preference for avoiding direct duplication of the Northern Line.

Stage 3 would see the new line merge north of Finsbury Park with an extension from the low-level Northern City Line terminus and continue in tube beneath the LNER line to Bowes Road, replacing the LNER stations at Harringay, Hornsey and Wood Green. The line would then surface and run on electrified LNER tracks towards Cuffley. North of Finsbury Park, junctions (similar to those at Camden Town on the Northern Line) would also allow part of the joint service to proceed in tube towards Seven Sisters and thence to Enfield Town.

The Development of the Route

The Second World War severely reduced planning work on any expansion of the Underground as more urgent tasks took precedence. However, wartime conditions did contrive to present certain opportunities. In October 1940 the government and LPTB discussed building a number of deep-level air-raid shelters with the possibility that after the war they could be incorporated into tube railway expansion schemes. The Board stated that they had only rough and not fully developed schemes in mind. It was therefore agreed that the shelter tunnels would be placed parallel with existing lines, not on speculative alignments of brand-new tubes. This would reduce the cost of duplicating overcrowded sections of railway after the war, should the need arise (as well as allowing the new tunnels to be linked to existing shelter stations). The proposals inevitably rekindled some of the pre-1939 development thinking where simple duplication of lines was favoured.

The sections immediately thought worthy of duplication were Camden Town to Tottenham Court Road, Kennington to Balham and Bank to Holborn. Shelters were therefore considered at Mornington Crescent, Warren Street, Goodge Street, Oval, Stockwell, Clapham North, Clapham Common, Clapham South, St Paul's and Chancery Lane, a total of ten. Later on, Mornington Crescent and Warren Street shelters were dropped in favour of others at Belsize Park and Camden Town; Oval was started but not completed and St Paul's was not built. Each comprised 1200ft (364m) twin tunnel sections some 16ft (4.8m) diameter. In the context of late 1930s plans some shelters were conveniently sited for a future South London–Victoria–Finsbury Park tube.

The next hint at future developments appears to have been in 1943 in a document produced by the Ministry of War Transport. This appeared under the hand of Colonel Alan Mount, Chief Inspecting Officer of Railways to the Ministry, and sets out for consideration the development of railway facilities in post-war Britain.

Colonel Mount favoured the 'Finsbury Park to Victoria' tube, with a southern alignment continuing on to meet and then follow the 'express' Northern Line scheme to Morden (but now with a possible extension to Cheam); north of Finsbury Park the preferred alignment remained towards Bowes Park and thence (unspecifically) on to the LNER system. However, the central London alignment reverted to the route via Tottenham Court Road, and the Great Portland Street objective appears to have been lost. While this is not explained, the other main work was a return to the Victoria–Cricklewood scheme (rather than the more ambitious 1939 proposals) and this effectively duplicated much of the Victoria–Great Portland Street route.

A development from the 1939 scheme (and the statements made in connection with the deep shelters in 1940) now acknowledged that the overcrowding on the Northern Line actually began north of Camden Town. An ambitious scheme was thus suggested whereby that line would be entirely duplicated between Golders Green and Morden by an express tube. The existence of the wartime shelter tunnels may have swayed Mount's thinking. If this option were pursued then it was proposed that the separate Finsbury Park–Tottenham Court Road–Victoria–Morden proposal would be curtailed at an exchange station at Clapham Common. An express tube following the Central Line west of Liverpool Street was still being considered, though now extended farther west, to Wood Lane.

Equally optimistic planning, on an even grander scale, was unveiled in 1943 as the County of London Plan, devised by J. H. Forshaw, Superintending Architect to the London County Council, assisted by Sir Patrick Abercrombie. It followed the prevailing ideology among architects by proposing the drastic rebuilding of much of London, both to group activities by zone and to cope with traffic growth. Major expansion of the Underground was not favoured, interconnection between the main line railways being preferred. Extensive proposals were made for a scheme of interlinked loop tunnels under central London for main line trains; these satisfied the current desire to replace the Thames railway bridges so abhorrent to the architectural profession.

While the County of London Plan gave a psychological boost to a city still at war, its practicability was less inspiring during the period of post-war austerity. Other, more modest, plans soon superseded the 1943 ideas. But one of the Plan's more useful suggestions had already been acted upon. It had proposed the setting up of a committee specifically to look at the railway implications of the plan and to produce detailed proposals. The recommendation was adopted and the Railway (London Plan) Committee was appointed on 22nd February 1944.

The Committee was a substantially railway-orientated body that included Colonel (and by now Sir) Alan Mount and representatives of the LPTB and the main line companies. In its first report of 21st January 1946 a somewhat jaundiced view was taken of the proposals for the demise of the railway bridges and recommendations were formulated which bore an interesting resemblance to the Ministry's 1943 plan. The Finsbury Park to Victoria link survived, albeit somewhat adjusted, as *Route 8* in the proposed plan.

Major changes between the 1946 plan and its forebears included dropping the Central Line express tube in favour of independent east–west tubes and diversion of the Cricklewood tube away from Victoria towards Charing Cross, Cannon Street and London Bridge. The duplication of the Northern Line from at least Camden Town to Morden was allowed for, with the section from Kennington to Tooting regarded as urgent.

With wholesale duplication of the Northern Line now being suggested, the central London routeing of the Victoria–Finsbury Park proposal (*Route 8*) no longer needed to do the same thing, which resulted in it being shifted westwards, to tackle different traffic flows. These were principally some of the most heavily used existing connections, such as the Victoria–Euston and Victoria–King's Cross traffics. Similarly, journeys from Victoria to Mayfair and Oxford Street were circuitous and it was desired to reduce the pressure of traffic at Victoria (District Line) station and interchange traffic at Tottenham Court Road and Leicester Square. The revised central London route therefore became King's Cross, Euston, Bond Street and Hyde Park Corner to Victoria.

North of Finsbury Park, *Route 8* remained aimed towards Bowes Park to join the LNER with a view to running over newly electrified tracks northwards (the actual limit of running was still not precisely defined). South of Victoria *Route 8* no longer needed to make a link at Kennington and a route to East Croydon via Vauxhall, Stockwell (Northern Line interchange), Brixton, Streatham and Norbury was proposed instead, the line running at surface level beyond Norbury. The section from Croydon to Finsbury Park was to be 14 miles (22.4km) long and the expected cost was then £24 million. It had been recommended that the new tube be built to a new standard which allowed for 17ft (5.2m) diameter tunnels (main line size) with platforms 16ft (4.9m) wide and 650ft (198m) long – nearly double the length of existing platforms, and long enough for 12-car trains. The numerous schemes recommended by the Committee were divided into four levels of priority and *Route 8* was given the status of a first priority work 'to meet immediate traffic requirements'. It might be mentioned that against this planning background the Standing Joint Committee of the Board and main line railways still existed and met several times during 1946 to look at post-war investment priorities. Almost perversely it was slow to contribute to the debate on the London Plan tubes, although it did eventually acknowledge the usefulness of *Route 8*, but thought the southern end could be turned west as an express railway serving the Osterley World Fair in 1951, and thence London Airport (Heathrow).

In contrast, the LPTB, even in its final year of existence, adopted a very positive approach. It evaluated with enthusiasm the various prevailing schemes, and by February 1947 had put together a detailed draft plan largely based on the London Plan Committee's proposals. *Route 8* was favoured, but in a modified form which was termed *Scheme D*. In central London a revised route took the line via Green Park and Oxford Circus stations, instead of Hyde Park Corner and Bond Street. This was felt a substantially better option which allowed same-level interchange with the Bakerloo Line at Oxford Circus. This station was quite inadequate for the prevailing traffic and had an inefficient and congested layout – so much so that it had previously been thought to make impractical the addition of a new line with same-level interchange. Nevertheless a scheme had been devised although it was only possible if *Scheme D* was of conventional 12ft (3.8m) bore and not the 17ft (5.2m) bore intended for *Route 8*; almost total reconstruction of the station was also required. A small bore line would restrict the opportunities for through running on to the main line system but it would significantly reduce costs, perhaps even to the point of affordability.

To the south of Victoria, *Scheme D* was not greatly dissimilar to *Route 8* except that it was proposed to extend to West (instead of East) Croydon and thence beyond at surface level to South Croydon where the line would bifurcate to branches for Coulsdon North and Sanderstead.

North of Finsbury Park, *Scheme D* was quite different from *Route 8* and reflected a complete rethink about how the LNER branch and main line services could be improved. It was proposed to extend the new tube line north-eastwards to Seven Sisters where it would split into two branches, one to Hoe Street (in Walthamstow) and the other to Tottenham Hale from which point trains would be projected at surface level to Waltham Cross. One of the main objectives in doing this was to intercept nearly all radial and orbital lines in that sector of London. Thus interchanges with the Chingford branch would be made at Hoe Street, the Tottenham loop line at Blackhorse Road, the Waltham Cross line by direct service, the Enfield Town and Palace Gates branches at Seven Sisters, the Piccadilly Line at Manor House, the LNER main line and Northern Line at Finsbury Park and the North London Line at Barnsbury. A 36 trains per hour maximum service was proposed on the main section of the line with 18 trains per hour on the branches (except north of Tottenham Hale where six were proposed).

While London Transport was examining its response to the Working Party's report of 1946 there were major administrative changes looming. During the war both the LPTB and main line companies had been placed under government control; in practice the control was exercised by means of a Railway Executive Committee. This arrangement continued after the war, during which time the new government decided

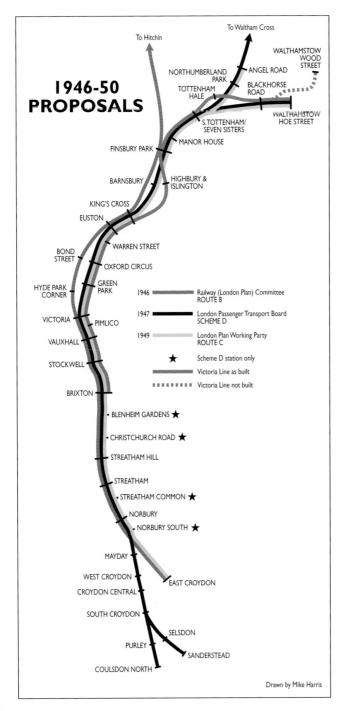

1946-50 PROPOSALS

To Hitchin

To Waltham Cross

WALTHAMSTOW WOOD STREET

NORTHUMBERLAND PARK

ANGEL ROAD

TOTTENHAM HALE

BLACKHORSE ROAD

S.TOTTENHAM/ SEVEN SISTERS

WALTHAMSTOW HOE STREET

MANOR HOUSE

FINSBURY PARK

BARNSBURY

HIGHBURY & ISLINGTON

KING'S CROSS

EUSTON

WARREN STREET

BOND STREET

OXFORD CIRCUS

HYDE PARK CORNER

GREEN PARK

VICTORIA

PIMLICO

VAUXHALL

STOCKWELL

BRIXTON

BLENHEIM GARDENS ★

CHRISTCHURCH ROAD ★

STREATHAM HILL

STREATHAM

STREATHAM COMMON ★

NORBURY

NORBURY SOUTH ★

MAYDAY

WEST CROYDON

EAST CROYDON

CROYDON CENTRAL

SOUTH CROYDON

SELSDON

PURLEY

SANDERSTEAD

COULSDON NORTH

1946		Railway (London Plan) Committee ROUTE 8
1947		London Passenger Transport Board SCHEME D
1949		London Plan Working Party ROUTE C
	★	Scheme D station only
		Victoria Line as built
	▪▪▪▪▪▪▪▪	Victoria Line not built

Drawn by Mike Harris

This map shows the plans considered during the 1946-49 period and may be seen to be a development of the pre-war Victoria to Finsbury Park schemes. Route C and Scheme D stations were not precisely defined except for interchange with Eastern Region.

upon the nationalisation of inland public transport. The system was to be vested in a body called the British Transport Commission (BTC), which effectively superseded the Railway Executive Committee. Separate statutory executive bodies were established in order to run the various arms of the business. Ironically, common ownership spelled the end of the London revenue pool and the manner of the planning process that went with it, the new executives largely working in isolation, vying with each other for scarce capital funds. On 1st January 1948 the London Passenger Transport Board thus passed to the London Transport Executive (LT), while the main line railways passed to the Railway Executive (British Railways, or BR).

The political and administrative upheaval inevitably clouded the issue of future planning. As a result, on 1st April 1948, the Chairman of the Commission advised the Minister of Transport that he had set up a working party to examine the proposals of the Railway (London Plan) Committee "in the light of the latest economic and other developments". Its report was published in 1949.

It was inevitable that the new Working Party would take on board the detailed examinations already made, and not perhaps surprising that it came out strongly in favour of building *Route 8*, but incorporating nearly all the modifications already suggested by London Transport in their *Scheme D*. The result was a specific proposal to build a new 12ft diameter tube railway, this time referred to as *Route C*. The Working Party saw no reason to deviate from the London Plan proposals at the Croydon end, so favoured East Croydon as the terminus. At the northern end of the line the Working Party preferred a tube line from Seven Sisters northwards only as far as an interchange with the BR Eastern Region at Angel Road, on the Waltham Cross line; this line was in any case the subject of a separate electrification proposal.

An optional branch line from Seven Sisters to Walthamstow Hoe Street via Blackhorse Road was given the status 'possibly desirable'. *Route C* as a whole was described as 'a most important traffic route' and was included among the four most urgent schemes to proceed.

The London Plan Working Party continued to meet under BTC auspices after the publication of their main report and made observations as appropriate. The grand schemes formulated in the 1940s gradually evaporated in the light of post-war reality where cash and materials shortages prevented even the proper maintenance of existing facilities. The prospect of massive new investment on additional schemes took on an air of an improbable dream. Nearly all the proposals were eventually dropped; only the most pressing were kept alive, these being *Route C* (north-east London to Croydon, just described) and phase 1 of another line, *Route D* (a west to north-east London scheme via Victoria and Fleet Street). Planning continued on this basis even though funding seemed impossible.

By 1951 the Working Party had concluded that the northern end of *Route C* should only serve the proposed 'branch' service to Blackhorse Road and Walthamstow. By diverting this branch via Tottenham Hale it was possible to retain interchange with the Waltham Cross line, though by escalators rather than by a direct service. Walthamstow was now felt better to be served by a station in the town centre at Hoe Street, and with a same-level interchange with the Chingford branch service at Wood Street station. By this time it had become the long-term objective to electrify the Eastern Region suburban services to Enfield and Chingford (though detailed proposals were not made until 1955). The Finsbury Park to Victoria routeing remained substantially unchanged. The layout at Wood Street envisaged *Route C* surfacing between the main line tracks a little to the west of the station, rising steeply to cross Wood Street on an overbridge then running into twin island platforms where the tube served the inner faces and the main line the outer ones. Beyond the station were to be seven (later six) stabling sidings.

The Wood Street plan just described (dated 1950) also included provision for *Route C* trains switching across to the Eastern Region tracks to allow a proportion of the service to continue to Chingford to take pressure off the existing steam service – it seems this was an option rather than the plan. It is evident that LT planners were convinced that a better solution would be to divert the entire Chingford service on to *Route C*. This could be accomplished by diverting the service beyond Tottenham Hale onto the Chingford branch just short of Walthamstow St James' Street station (moving it away from the Blackhorse Road alignment). Even as late as September 1953 LT harboured designs on adopting the Chingford line but there was very little enthusiasm from the Eastern Region who were planning their own electrification scheme (the addition of Chingford to either the LT or Eastern Region proposals would strengthen their respective financial cases and were therefore to an increasing extent rivals). In the end the urgency to brief the engineers and legal staff in October 1953 meant that Chingford aspirations had to be dropped permanently from *Route C*.

Map showing the authorised 'Route C' in relation to other railways.

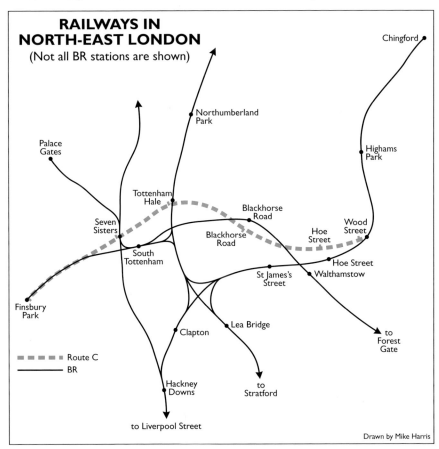

Diagram showing 'Route C' c.1950 while the northern terminals were not yet settled and Highbury and Warren Street were not yet included. At this stage Route C would have had interchange with the Piccadilly Line at Manor House. Later it was intended that Manor House would be served by Route C only and the Piccadilly Line be diverted to run direct between Finsbury Park and Turnpike Lane.

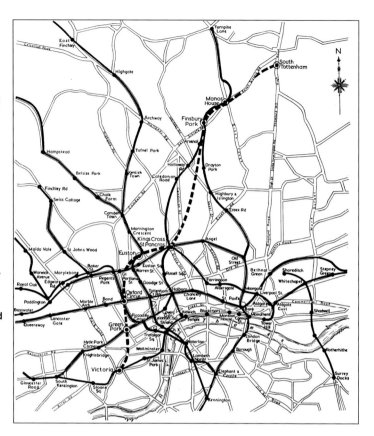

For the next couple of years, considerable work took place on more detailed planning and in reconciling innumerable conflicting factors (including tunnel diameter – 14ft 6ins (4.4m) was briefly considered possible). During this time LT arranged for an aerial survey of this route (and two others) to be undertaken preparatory to full scale engineering surveys. There were several issues that needed to be resolved. As originally promoted *Route C* was to run direct from King's Cross to Finsbury Park, which was an extremely long distance for a tube line to operate with no intermediate station (though a station at Barnsbury had at one time been mooted).

It must be recalled that the 1949 London Plan Working Party's report assumed completion of the partly-constructed pre-war works connecting the Northern City at Drayton Park with new high-level platforms at Finsbury Park (alongside the main line station), and with electrification of the Northern Heights branch to Highgate and Alexandra Palace, for through tube trains from Moorgate via Highbury & Islington. Although that scheme envisaged part of the Northern City service still terminating in the low-level platforms at Finsbury Park, it was felt there would be little problem in diverting the whole service to the upper platforms, releasing the tube station for *Route C* trains. By the time detailed engineering plans were drawn up for *Route C*, matters had become complicated by the abandonment of the Northern City extensions with the result that its trains all continued to use the low-level station. While there were now proposals to electrify the BR suburban services through Finsbury Park high-level, with local trains routed on to the main-line size Northern City (so vacating its low-level platforms), nobody could forecast when this might happen. If Route C were to be authorised before BR electrification, interim arrangements would be needed for the Northern City Line.

One option was to finish the pre-war link to Finsbury Park high-level, including the new platforms whose steelwork had already been erected (and, as late as 1962, retained at LT's request). This work might have a short life if the electrification later went ahead. Either way, the value of good interchange with Route C (to give a route to the City) was now considered paramount, and a plan was formulated for the diversion of Route C via Highbury & Islington where cross-platform interchange could be provided. Another (cheaper) option was simply to curtail the Northern City at Drayton Park and to divert passengers to other routes (including an interchange with the Route C at Highbury & Islington). Regardless of any interim arrangements, it was decided in principle that the Northern City low-level platforms at Finsbury Park had to be taken over.

The existing Piccadilly and Northern City platforms were parallel but independent of each other but by re-arranging the approach tracks it was possible to permit same-level interchange between the like directions of flow of the Piccadilly Line and Route C. To achieve this the southbound Piccadilly Line had necessarily to be diverted through the former northbound Northern City Line platform and Route C would then use the former southbound Northern City and the vacated southbound Piccadilly Line station tunnels. The Northern City Line was isolated from the rest of the Underground network and an option that received more than a little consideration was to retain the tunnels north of Drayton Park and provide running connections with the Victoria Line for empty stock movements; by this means Northern City trains could be maintained at Northumberland Park. In the event the works this would have required were grossly disproportionate to the benefits realisable and no provision was made.

Although the decision to shift the route eastwards, via Highbury & Islington, had been taken in principle by 1951, it was far from final. Providing cross platform interchange was very expensive and by 1953 there was pressure to cut it out and look at a cheaper alternative with better benefits. In particular it was thought possible that more effective relief to the Piccadilly Line might be given, possibly allowing Holloway Road and Caledonian Road stations to be closed (which would speed up services). Two alternatives were examined: a station at Nag's Head (Holloway) and a station at the junction of Holloway and Caledonian Roads. Although the latter was eventually thought preferable, in the final analysis the advantages of cross-platform interchange at Highbury to provide attractive, same-level interchange with the Northern City Line for passengers from Route C's suburbs going to the City, and for West End passengers from Alexandra Palace (1951) or the electrified main line services (1955) won the day. In the event it was the 'Great Northern Electrics' of 1976 that received the benefit.

The exact route between Seven Sisters and Walthamstow was only settled in September 1953, shortly before parliamentary approval was sought. Two possible routes had been considered. One envisaged a line mainly in tube tunnel from Seven Sisters that broke surface just short of Wood Street station. The second route saw the line breaking surface just south of Seven Sisters where it would run into a new station combining Seven Sisters and South Tottenham; it would then continue at surface level beside the Tottenham & Forest Gate line to Blackhorse Road, thence in tube, and as the first scheme to Wood Street. Both schemes anticipated intermediate Route C stations at

Blackhorse Road and in Walthamstow (Hoe Street). The tube route required a depot site to the north of the line on marshland between Northumberland Park station and the Lockwood Reservoir. The surface route envisaged a depot on Walthamstow Marshes, just north of Clapton. After lengthy evaluation the decision to adopt the tube route turned on five factors. A depot near the Lea Valley reservoirs (near Coppermill Junction) was so prone to flooding that the whole vast site would need raising by 12 feet (3.5 m) which would produce high subsidence risk (the Northumberland Park location was also prone to flooding but this could be managed by flood walls). Property disturbance would be significant along a surface route. The tube route facilitated an interchange with the Cambridge line at Tottenham Hale station to be made (reflecting the Working Party's preference), this was not impossible to do with the surface alignment, but not in a way calculated to generate local traffic. A better station arrangement was possible at Seven Sisters – the tube alignment permitted the station to be double-ended. Finally the gradients on a surface alignment would be more severe.

In 1953 the Minister of Transport and Civil Aviation announced that he accepted *Route C* as a first priority work, 'to be undertaken when circumstances permitted', but there was no hint as to when this might be (other than not soon). By this time the likelihood of other new works had further receded, and several of the uncompleted Northern Line pre-war new works had been officially cancelled. None of this could have been particularly encouraging to those pressing for the new tube line, and it is clear that the inexorable process of planning perhaps lacked vigour.

As already mentioned, south of Victoria the ultimate objective for *Route C* had been Croydon, routed via Vauxhall, Stockwell, Brixton, Streatham and Norbury. In Croydon itself the alignment presented problems. BR Southern Region planners were most anxious that the line reached East Croydon to provide interchange with the main line to Brighton, which would mean that *Route C* would miss Croydon town centre unless severe curves were put in. The solution was to pursue the earlier thinking about dividing the end of the line, with one branch from West Croydon to East Croydon and the other from West Croydon to the town centre and South Croydon; a possible depot site was examined between Selsdon and Sanderstead.

For reasons that will become clear later the nature of *Route D* now needs to be described. The part considered more urgent was the electrification of the Eastern Region suburban lines to Chingford and Enfield Town, to which would be linked a main line sized tube railway from Victoria, Trafalgar Square, Aldwych, Bank to Hackney Downs where a junction would be made (the branches from Enfield and Chingford converged at Hackney Downs and the tube was intended to ease the serious capacity constraint). The Trafalgar Square to Bank section would parallel what was later to become known as the Fleet Line. It was recognised that Victoria was not an ideal place to terminate the new line and it was suggested that, as a somewhat lower priority, it should be extended westwards, perhaps via Knightsbridge, Kensington High Street, Olympia and then along the Uxbridge Road to Yeading. However as planning work progressed a more suitable western outlet presented itself. The District Line was heavily overloaded at its western end where the convergence of four branches meant none of them received the level of service really needed. By projecting *Route D* via Chelsea and linking it with the Wimbledon Branch it was not only possible to relieve the Wimbledon line itself, but also the Earl's Court to Victoria section of the District.

By a point no later than the end of 1953 it had become evident that by some strange inversion of priorities the need for a Victoria–Hackney tube had somewhat diminished

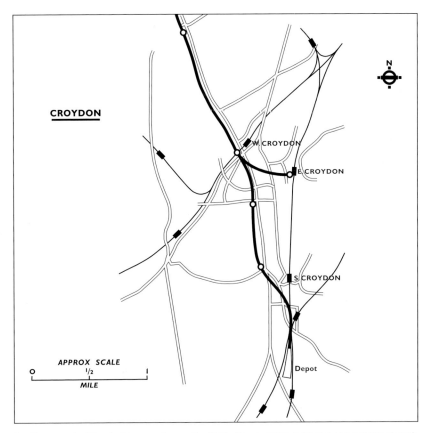

Southern end of 'Route C' as envisaged in 1951. All would be in tunnel except the depot approaches.

'Route C' map as at end of 1951 showing the possible temporary connection to the District Line's Wimbledon branch and the plan for the Piccadilly Line to be diverted away from Manor House.

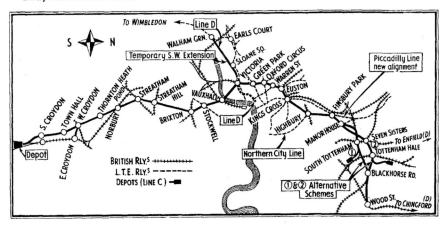

17

while relief for the District by means of a Victoria–Fulham link was now perceived as urgent. In fact it was considered more urgent than a southwards projection of *Route C* to Croydon. With this in mind London Transport began to think that in terms of best use of capital it would be better to project *Route C* to Fulham and Wimbledon on a purely temporary basis (it was far cheaper than Croydon) and when cash permitted (if it ever did) that section could be transferred to *Route D* and the southern *Route C* terminus switched to Croydon as originally planned. Some quite detailed planning proceeded on this basis, though government approval for projection south of Victoria stalled comprehensively. A complication of the Wimbledon scheme was that south of East Putney the tracks (owned by British Railways) carried Southern Region empty stock and diversionary passenger trains and it was feared the line would not have the capacity required for those and the District and *Route C* trains. Nevertheless resignalling and a new lay-by siding near Southfields were thought able to solve this.

By 1954, with government acceptance of the main scheme obtained in principle, and with the routeing of the line north of Victoria now settled, the BTC decided to seek parliamentary powers in their Bill of that year to construct the Victoria–Walthamstow section – the principal powers were therefore enshrined in the British Transport Commission Act 1955. While powers were being sought the *Route C* station at Manor House and the Piccadilly Line diversion were abandoned because of anticipated difficulties in staging the work, and because the station risked overloading the in-town section of the new line. The terminal alignment at Victoria suited future extension either towards Croydon or Chelsea and Fulham.

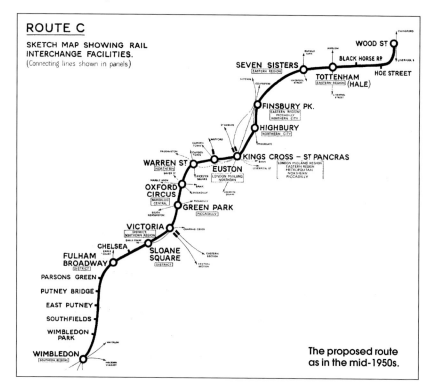

ROUTE C

SKETCH MAP SHOWING RAIL
INTERCHANGE FACILITIES.
(Connecting lines shown in panels)

The proposed route
as in the mid-1950s.

Detailed Planning and Authorisation

The parliamentary process undoubtedly transformed *Route C* from what could have been construed simply as a planner's dream into a scheme perceived as likely to be built. Indeed, it was not then long before the proposed line acquired a name – the Victoria Line – first mentioned tentatively in public by the Chairman, Sir John Elliot, in December 1955 and in the absence of anything better acquiring permanence.

Finding a name for the line had caused some difficulty. 'Viking Line' was a possibility toyed with, adopting the same principle used on the Baker-loo. The 'Walvic Line' was another unfortunate example. In the end the name 'Victoria Line' emerged early in 1955 during a meeting for that purpose between Sir John Elliot (the Chairman) and David McKenna (the Chief Commercial and Public Relations Officer). Geographical significance was sought but combinations of names – Kingvic was another – simply didn't work. After testing many other geographical propositions (including the 'Mayfair Line' and the 'West End Line') the name 'Victoria Line' was stumbled upon and sounded just right.

Whilst undoubtedly a milestone, the passing of an Act of Parliament in no way committed the BTC to pay for and build a new railway: the problem was how to finance the line. Prior to the Second World War money for expanding railways (including the LPTB) was supplied by private investors. These investors were rewarded by payments of interest the cost of which was paid for from the enhanced revenues from the expanded transport system. To make the interest payments affordable governments had sometimes guaranteed them, which allowed money to be borrowed more cheaply. Even when British transport was nationalised the BTC still had to borrow money for new works from the capital markets; those works were required as a very minimum to generate sufficient revenue to repay interest and in due course preferably the capital too. The BTC's financial position was deteriorating rapidly and the Victoria Line was not considered at all likely to 'pay its way' given its capital and operating costs.

It is worth looking at the financial forecasts of the mid nineteen-fifties to see quite where the sticking point arose. It was estimated that the Victoria Line would cost £50million to build. This represented works and equipment costs of £40million, with £2million for land and easements, £4million for rolling stock and £4million for plant and overheads. At the prevailing fixed interest rate of 4 per cent, the annual interest charges to the Commission would be some £2million.

It was estimated that the line would cost a million pounds a year to run. While traffic receipts were thought likely to exceed running costs by some £350,000 a year, it was realised that much of the traffic carried on the new line would be existing traffic which had diverted, so that over the system as a whole there would be a net deficit of about £250,000 a year. Added to the interest charges the line would therefore require some £2.25 million to be found at a time when the BTC was already making a heavy loss. Alternatively, in the context of annual fares revenue of £100million for all the BTC's London area services, the cost of the Victoria Line represented a fares increase of 2½ per cent (at that time for charging purposes the London area was considered a discrete unit where equal fares applied on all the BTC's services).

The issue was therefore very much a social one. The new tube was likely to be of considerable benefit to London. It would open up new areas to Underground travel, speed up numerous cross London journeys (especially between some main line termini), considerably ease congestion at many stations and overcrowded sections of line, and also relieve a certain amount of street congestion. The idea of charging its net revenue loss against fares was not liked within the BTC or London Transport, but the government were not prepared to make a capital grant towards tube railway construction from public funds although, even then, such grants were made for road construction.

Passenger levels had peaked in 1948 and while they later declined they mainly did so only outside the rush hours. Between 1939 and 1954 traffic arriving at Victoria main line station in the morning peak (7am to 10am) had increased by 40 per cent, but this hid the fact that the peak was becoming more concentrated – the increase in the heaviest hour was 75 per cent. The Underground station was unable to cope and the circuitous journeys available from Victoria (either by train or bus), and the poor interchanges at places like Charing Cross (now Embankment) resulted in vast numbers of people choosing to swarm across St James's Park rather than use public transport. Even so Victoria Underground was somehow carrying 27million passengers a year and was the busiest station on a single line. To carry this traffic away the section of District Line between Victoria and Charing Cross was somehow carrying 22,000 passengers in the busier direction in the busiest hour. The Victoria Line would reduce this to a more tolerable – but still busy – 15,000. The busiest section of the Underground was the Piccadilly south of Manor House at 23,000 per hour peak flow; the Victoria Line was to reduce this to 15,000. To achieve these ends the Victoria Line was to be built with the capacity to handle 8-car trains operating at the rate of 40 trains an hour south of Seven Sisters (where there was to be a reversing facility). However initial services were to be of 7-car trains operating a 32 trains an hour service (16 north of Seven Sisters); off-peak a 24 trains an hour service of 3- or 4-car trains was envisaged along the main section.

In December 1956 the BTC authorised LT to incur costs of up to £500,000 for detailed planning of the Victoria Line. Although there had already been some desultory property acquisition for working sites the BTC was determined not to suggest to the world at large that there was the slightest chance of the line being constructed without additional funding, and it was only with reluctance that even the money for planning was released (and even then it was spent painfully slowly).

The BTC had become so pessimistic about the line ever getting funded that it asked LT to consider staged options to make the project more digestible. A proposal evaluated by December 1956 was to build the Victoria to King's Cross portion only. This was not a proposal without complications. With no depot of its own it was considered necessary to construct a link with the Piccadilly north of King's Cross so that Victoria Line trains could be maintained at Cockfosters (twelve 7-car trains would be needed to operate a 24 trains an hour service). Furthermore it seemed possible that there would be a very serious interchange problem between the main line and the Victoria Line platforms because much heavier flows would exist than with the full scheme. A truncated line was expected to cost £23½million to build and equip (including the track connection) compared with what by then was thought to be a £51½million for the full scheme. Many of the line's benefits would not be achieved, including, of course, any benefits to north-east London.

An alternative idea simply to build a King's Cross–Tottenham section was quickly dismissed as of little benefit on its own. However a Victoria–Finsbury Park option was thought of value as it would achieve at least some benefits to north-east London, particularly the relief of the Piccadilly Line north of King's Cross. Although the physical link with the Piccadilly at Finsbury Park was much easier than at King's Cross the larger number of trains required to provide the service (at least 30) could not be accommodated at Cockfosters and this presented a major difficulty. More seriously the capital expenditure required was considerably more than for King's Cross alone and the additional benefits much fewer. LT considered only the first option had any merit at all, but were evidently disinclined to press for anything less than the complete line (no doubt fearing – and with some justification – that if a staged approach were adopted there would never be a stage 2). However, there was no more chance of getting support for a £22million scheme than one for £51million and the upshot was that no authority emerged for proceeding.

In 1958, with the government still stonewalling on its willingness to make any contribution, the scheme was reappraised. Various new developments needed to be taken into account, including the outcome of the 1958 bus strike which had altered commuter traffic patterns. As part of this two alternatives were considered to the full scheme (by now costed at £55million). A Victoria to Seven Sisters option could be achieved for £45.4million and the earlier Victoria to King's Cross option, by now £25.5million, including the Piccadilly link. However in January 1959, LT recommended sticking to the whole line as the savings in extending only to Seven Sisters were only about £10million but were attended with considerable loss of benefits, and the King's Cross option was considered unviable, especially as LT were by now planning tunnelling experiments near Finsbury Park to validate the potential for new lower-cost tunnelling techniques and the works would be wasted if the line stopped at King's Cross. LT's hard-line view was there was no realistic low-cost option.

In 1959 the London Travel Committee examined the Victoria Line against a background of travel improvements of comparable costs; the Victoria Line came out exceedingly well. The Committee reported to the Minister that the "Victoria Line as it is at present planned should be authorised forthwith and construction put in hand as quickly as possible". The recommendation cut no ice.

Meanwhile, as already hinted, London Transport had decided to make a detailed study of the latest tunnelling techniques to take account of the significant improvements that had been made since its last involvement with extensive railway tunnelling some twenty years previously.

A particular technical advance had been made in the form of a machine called the 'drum digger'. This had just been used on a remarkable 19 mile (30km) long, 8ft 6ins (2.6m) internal diameter tunnel built by the Metropolitan Water Board between Hampton and the Lea Valley reservoirs. The machine consisted of the usual cylindrical shield that was pushed forward by hydraulic rams, the space behind each thrust then being lined by the tunnel lining segments. At the leading edge of the shield was erected a rotating, circular framework to which cutting teeth were fixed. In turn, the cutting framework was attached to a rotating drum, somewhat smaller than the surrounding shield, and through the centre of which the clay spoil tumbled to be carried away by conveyor to portable skips. A maximum tunnelling speed of 400 feet (120m) per week had been achieved and a scaled-up drum digger appeared to suit the needs of Victoria Line construction.

Tunnel linings, too, had developed substantially since the earliest days of tube railways. These had long been built with cast-iron segmental linings bolted together, with the cavity between the lining and surrounding clay filled under pressure by a cement grouting. This system had a number of disadvantages and in 1949 experiments began with an iron tunnel lining where the segments were expanded against the clay such that they then locked together by compression of the clay acting on the completed tunnel. There were many problems to be overcome, but in 1958 a 14ft (4.27m) diameter shield-driven tunnel was being built at Belvedere Power Station by the Central Electricity Generating Board, and at LT's expense 20 rings of unbolted iron-lining was erected. This showed that the lining itself was successful and that it was possible to handle and erect the segments satisfactorily.

It had proved expedient while building the eastern extension of the Central Line between 1937 and 1939 to experiment with reinforced concrete linings using pre-cast segments that were otherwise similar to the traditional iron ones. This type of tunnel had proved slightly more awkward to build, but was cheaper and showed the utility of concrete. For the Victoria Line the cost of concrete tunnels appeared attractive. In any case there were doubts as to whether sufficient iron segments could be made available to furnish the whole of the new line and it was therefore desired to try unbolted, compression-locked concrete segments. Again the Thames–Lea tunnel offered practical experience with such linings and the unbolted concrete segments used there proved highly successful.

In order to test the new types of tunnelling machines and tunnel linings it was decided to utilise the 1955 parliamentary powers to construct a one mile (1.6km) length of experimental twin tunnel from Finsbury Park to South Tottenham. Half a million pounds had been put aside by the Commission in 1956 specifically for this work,

Example of concrete-lined tunnel tested in the experimental section north of Finsbury Park built in 1960/61. In this type of tunnel the segments were held together by the compression of the surrounding ground. Prominent in this picture are the side ledges intended mainly to keep wheel-rail sound below car floor level. LT Museum

but this was later doubled. Government authority to build the experimental tunnel was given in 1959 and it was started in January 1960. Working shafts were sunk in Finsbury Park, next to the Eastern Region main line, and at Netherton Road, at the corner of Seven Sisters Road. Once the shafts were sunk tunnel drives were started using drum diggers, the tunnelling teams working towards each other. The intention was that the tunnel drives would meet at a point near Manor House Piccadilly Line station.

The northern section (Manor House to Netherton Road) was built using unbolted cast-iron segments of 12ft 6ins (3.8m) minimum internal diameter, the drum digger shield having an outside diameter of 13ft 1ins (4.0m). The southern section of tunnel (Finsbury Park to Manor House) used a larger drum digger, of 14ft (4.3m) diameter, for use with concrete tunnel linings, which were thicker than the iron ones. The concrete lined tunnels used pre-cast segments that interlocked. Although several thicknesses of segments were tried varying from 4½ to 9 inches (115–230mm), 6 inch (150mm) thick segments proved to be the best compromise between economy and the sturdiness required for handling. The internal diameter chosen, and the smooth internal finish of the concrete, was thought likely to reduce significantly the drag on the train due to air resistance, and hence save energy. By March 1961 one of the bores was complete from Finsbury Park to Manor House, and the other from Manor House to Netherton Road; a cross-passage was built at Manor House to link the two tunnels and to allow accurate surveys to be transferred between them. The cross-passage was later incorporated into an access tunnel leading from a shaft sunk at the site of Manor House substation. The tunnelling was completed in July 1961 and illustrated that a tunnelling speed of 60 feet (18m) a day could be achieved in favourable conditions, which was substantially faster than older methods of construction.

Example of 'articulated' iron-lined tunnel tested in the experimental section north of Finsbury Park. Like the concrete tunnels these segments interlocked and relied on ground pressure to maintain integrity. Conventional bolted cast-iron segments were also used on parts of the line. LT Museum

The future southbound experimental tunnel was then extended from the cross passage at the Finsbury Park shaft to make an end-on junction with the southbound Northern City Line just north of Finsbury Park station. Track was then laid along about 1600 feet (490m) of the new tunnel and was connected the Northern City Line, which allowed the latter's pre-1938 stock trains to be used for vibration, ventilation and other tests in the experimental tunnel to which it was connected. The trackwork in the new tunnel was available for test purposes from Sunday 13th May 1962.

Desperate to contain costs, various interested authorities continued to seek economies. In response to civil service probing during 1960 LT had to reinvestigate the case for abandoning the section north of Seven Sisters (as well as the case for not constructing the line at all), and as late as 1961 the case for constructing Blackhorse Road was subject to scrutiny.

At last, on 20th August 1962, the government announced that the new tube could proceed. The breakthrough was influenced by a government-commissioned report by two Oxford academics, C. D. Foster and M. E. Beesley, which took factors other than simple finance into account; in other words a cost-benefit analysis. This demonstrated that the social benefits of the Victoria Line would more than justify spending the money required – on a social benefit basis the line (far from making a loss) would generate an 11.3 per cent rate of return. The cost was now some £56million to be financed by advances of a government loan (LT explained that if the new line were not built then £8million would need to be spent anyway on station reconstruction: this was an interesting statement given that eight years previously LT categorically stated it was not prepared to make heavy investment in station enlargement likely to be of use for merely three hours a day). The interest charges were inevitably to be set against higher fares, an arrangement which evoked some criticism in the press, much comparison being drawn with the systems in other major cities where governments at least paid for the running tunnels. Today the 'social benefit' element at the very least would be provided in the form of a government grant but at that time the only way of restricting the source of such subsidy to Londoners was a fares increase, the government's actual contribution being merely to absorb the political fall-out. It was a point of some debate that the benefits of the new line would be enjoyed by many others than Londoners but governments of all shades had had an especial phobia of providing capital grants for railways – that had a means of collecting their own revenues – as against roads that had no such means and where capital expenditure took place on a vast scale.

Other factors weighing in favour of the timing included the possibility of showing a political commitment to the new London Transport Board; although this did not take charge until 1st January 1963 it was set up as a result of the 1962 Transport Act which received the Royal Assent on 1st August 1962, only nineteen days prior to Victoria Line authorisation. The unemployment situation was also unfavourable to the government of the day and there was a suggestion that constructing the Victoria Line could create a usefully large number of new jobs.

Later studies into the delays before authorisation conclude that the London Transport Executive did everything reasonably possible to persuade the authorities that an early start was needed urgently. However the Executive had always to work through the BTC where it is suggested that the sense of urgency was somewhat diluted; a possible result of perceiving a risk that the Victoria Line might be authorised at the expense of the British Railways' modernisation programme, which was of more direct interest. This may especially have been so while London Transport's image was a very good one while that of British Railways was rather decrepit.

London Transport's chairman, Alec Valentine, suggested in 1965 that useful movement in the direction of building (rather than discussing) the line only happened when LT began direct negotiations with the Ministry of Transport during 1961, when the Transport Bill was being prepared. He felt that the Ministry thereby gained a more intimate grasp of the needs and problems of London Transport, and the Victoria Line was an early result.

The Ministry's view was not wholly in accord with that of Valentine. It preferred to suggest that the Victoria Line case was a marginal one in financial terms and that in the battle for capital investment it found difficulty in getting sufficiently near the top of the list. It was finally approved for other reasons, said the Permanent Secretary, though he did not cite political expediency as one of them! But there was common ground between Valentine and the Ministry in observing that the Victoria Line fared quite well in London Transport terms, but not in terms of the Commission as a whole; so whatever other factors were at play, the demise of the BTC is one of undoubted significance.

There remains at the moment plenty of room for discussion about the exact timing of the government go-ahead, nearly 25 years after J. P. Thomas originally perceived the need and usefulness of new tubes in central London. For example, another factor had been the comparatively recent introduction of rolling programmes of capital investment in which Victoria Line expenditure became less unfavourable than it did when specific ad hoc annual bids had to be made for the necessary money.

When authority did arrive it caused a dilemma. A feature of the continual hints of 'soon, but not now' was that it was impracticable to keep updating the station designs, with attendant survey and parliamentary costs. Unless considerable further delay was to be caused, the seven-year-old plans for the station civil engineering had to be utilised, although recognised no longer to be ideal. This was to cause serious problems many years later and was a very different approach from that of the recent extension of the Jubilee Line where the stations have been designed to be as large as is reasonably practical to be future-proof for perhaps a century.

An important preliminary to building the new line was to check the nature of the ground through which tunnelling would take place. This was achieved by means of trial borings. This view shows a trial boring taking place from within Green Park. Capital Transport

The Route Described

The preferred tunnel arrangement was one where the stations were built on 'humps' in the track; the gradients tending to slow trains down when approaching platforms, and accelerate them when leaving, resulting in a useful energy saving. Except in a very few instances this was very difficult to do on the Victoria Line where the level rose 130 feet (40m) between Victoria and Finsbury Park, then dropped 100 feet (30m) beneath the Lea Valley before recovering this level again at Wood Street (as the original plan allowed). Furthermore the levels at certain intermediate stations were also fixed by existing conditions, such as underground structures or the requirements for same-level interchange.

Before describing the detailed construction of the Victoria Line it will be helpful to examine the authorised route and to look at some of the difficulties that it presented, especially at the north end.

The parliamentary powers allowed for the new railway to surface at Wood Street station to provide cross-platform interchange with Chingford services, with sidings beyond the station for Victoria Line trains to reverse and stable. However, the Chingford line electrification had been completed by November 1960, on the overhead line system, and it was stated that the disruption caused by the construction of the Victoria Line would have been unacceptable. It might be borne in mind that the electrification had not got off to a good start and had been plagued by rolling stock problems that prevented the full service being introduced. Traffic had also increased on the Chingford line and for all these reasons it was decided to review the revised traffic needs and costs of sending the Victoria Line to Wood Street. By the end of 1961 it had been decided to abandon the section from Hoe Street to Wood Street. It might perhaps be added that truncating the line, together with a cheaper tunnelling estimate resulting from the experimental work, cut out £4million of the £5million increase in costs between 1958 and 1961, and was a factor in the line being given the go-ahead.

The initially-authorised site for Hoe Street station was at the junction of Hoe Street, High Street and Church Hill. With the loss of the Wood Street portion it was possible to re-align Hoe Street platforms so that they would run under the Eastern Region station instead; interchange with the Chingford line was thus maintained. Authority for the changes was granted in the British Transport Commission Act 1963. The result was a Victoria Line station reached by steps linking the main line platforms to an intermediate concourse, whence escalators led to the tube platforms. Tickets were to be issued and collected by BR staff from the main line station ticket office, which was modernised. The result was a triumph of economy over perfection, with the Victoria Line access available only by walking along the main line platforms but 'within barrier' interchange was possible and outside the railway station a new bus station was constructed with a feeder bus network planned.

The next station was to be at Blackhorse Road, across the road from the existing BR station. Interchange was thus notional (and was not advertised as such at first) but for the number of passengers that would have benefited the costs were adjudged too high.

It was planned to be a simple two-platform station with the escalators from the street level ticket hall coming down between the platforms. The line then veered almost north-west in order to reach Tottenham Hale. This station would be similar to Blackhorse Road but the ticket hall also served the Eastern Region Cambridge line platforms.

The depot site was near BR's Northumberland Park station on the Cambridge line, and the land taken was effectively waste marshland that required extensive draining. A mile-long twin tube connection took the line to the surface where siding and repair facilities were to be available for the whole line.

Seven Sisters station was to have three platforms, the middle one of which was primarily intended to serve trains terminating there. Although it had long been the intention to reverse a proportion of the service at Seven Sisters, it was now proposed that the access tracks to and from the depot join the sidings north of the station, replacing the authorised proposal for this connection to be made north of Tottenham Hale (the change was allowed in the British Transport Commission Act 1957). The station was to have escalators at each end of the platforms, one set leading to the BR station in the High Road, where a new joint ticket hall would be built, and the other leading to a concourse beneath the junction of the High Road and Seven Sisters Road.

The first Underground map to show the new line was printed at the end of 1962.

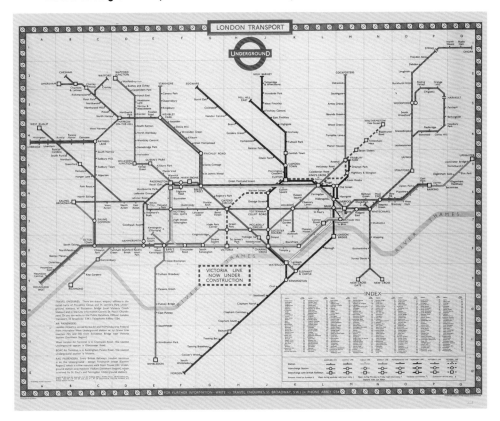

27

Trains from the middle road could proceed either to the depot or to Walthamstow, but all reversing trains had to proceed north of the station to reverse in either of the depot access roads and then come back to the southbound platform.

South of Seven Sisters the line would continue in twin tubes beneath the Seven Sisters Road towards Finsbury Park where the existing Northern City Line low-level platforms were to be taken over. The angst concerning the Finsbury Park to King's Cross routeing via Highbury has already been referred to. At Finsbury Park the Northern City Line had to be evicted and would release two parallel tube platforms which would be used by Piccadilly and Victoria Line southbound services. The construction arrangements will be referred to later, but suffice to say here that this was to mean there would be separate entrances/exits to the northbound and southbound sides of the station reached via the existing long and dreary subways buried under the main line station. Access to the main line platforms could be made by separate, equally dreary, spiral stairways. With money extremely tight there was little else that could be done.

Same-level interchange at Highbury required construction of two additional platforms. The northbound Northern City Line was to be re-routed through one of them and was engineered for main-line gauge trains in anticipation of the Eastern Region electrification scheme. The other one, together with the vacated Northern City platform, were destined for the Victoria Line. All four platforms would be linked to a low-level concourse by steps, and then by escalators to a new surface building over the BR North London Line tracks, giving a new interchange facility with that line. The existing BR ticket hall and the Northern City street-level station and lifts would be closed.

At King's Cross the complexity of existing railway tunnels permitted only one site for the Victoria Line platforms. The new line had to thread its way above the Piccadilly Line but just below the tunnels carrying the British Railways services to Moorgate via the Metropolitan 'Widened Lines'; this extremely congested site was one reason why running tunnels were constrained to 12ft (3.6m) diameter: there was not the room to build anything bigger at reasonable cost. There was to be a reversing siding just north of the station which would otherwise be of the usual twin platform arrangement with escalators leading up to the existing Northern Line and Piccadilly Line ticket hall, which would be enlarged; a low-level stairway also linked the Victoria Line with these tube lines.

At Euston same-level interchange was sought with the Northern Line (City branch), whose existing tracks shared a single large-bore station tunnel and flanked a narrow island platform with an access at one end leading to the three ageing lifts and the Northern Line (Charing Cross branch) platforms. The arrival of the Victoria Line meant that the existing station tunnel would remain to serve just southbound Northern Line trains while the northbound service would be diverted through a 2500ft (760m) diversion tunnel serving a new northbound platform. The Victoria Line would thread its way between the two Northern Line platforms to provide the same-level interchange. Both the Victoria and Northern Lines ran east–west at Euston, so an odd result of providing same-level, same direction interchange was that southbound trains faced the opposite way on each line (and likewise northbound). Such interchange also required the Victoria Line to adopt 'right-hand running' through Euston, but practical considerations dictated that the tunnels 'rolled over' each other north of King's Cross, and back again south of Warren Street, so 'wrong direction' running prevailed at these stations too.

Engineering at Euston was further complicated because prior to Victoria Line authorisation the BTC was planning wholesale reconstruction of the main line station above. The three 80 year old lifts might not survive the considerable strain upon them if they had to last until the new station facilities were entirely ready. It was decided to build a new entrance, ticket hall and escalator shaft to the Charing Cross branch platforms to relieve pressure on the existing lifts and ticket hall. The new facilities would be built to allow incorporation into the planned Victoria Line works – if and when they were authorised. Work began on a temporary entrance and a pair of escalators towards the end of 1961; these came into use on 8th March 1965 (with main entrance via what is now the suburban lines entrance by platforms 8–11, at that time briefly the barrier line for all of the main line platforms). Initially the new entrance was only used between 6am and 8pm and the older entrance remained open throughout the day, though now with only two lifts available. The Victoria Line go-ahead in August 1962 meant the eventual installation of a further six escalators and closure of the old ticket hall and lifts.

A change was made on the Euston to Oxford Circus section in diverting the Victoria Line via Warren Street station; this was done on the grounds that it broke an otherwise lengthy section of line in central London and improved public transport access to an increasingly important area. Warren Street was to comprise a simple pair of platforms with escalators leading up to an existing intermediate level between two flights of Northern Line escalators. To increase capacity a third escalator was to replace the fixed stairway in the upper Northern Line flight, now to serve both lines. The ticket hall area was re-arranged but little other alteration was made to the station.

Oxford Circus required comprehensive redevelopment. Throughout the 1950s the station was unable to cope satisfactorily with its existing peak hour traffic and it was inconceivable to contemplate any additional load without wholesale reconstruction. A new ticket hall beneath the 'circus' itself and several new banks of escalators were therefore planned, together with major new low-level subways. Same-level interchange with the Bakerloo Line was a paramount requirement; fortunately the existing Bakerloo platforms were 'outside' the tracks, and this made the design of the interchange with the Victoria Line more straightforward.

Green Park was to be a simple two-platform arrangement with escalators leading up to the existing (though much enlarged) ticket hall. At low level a long and tedious subway connection would link the Victoria and Piccadilly Lines.

Victoria station presented a different problem for the planners. We have already seen that the 1949 plan contemplated the new line continuing southward towards Croydon and that this was still an option being advocated under the *Route C* banner in 1951. We have also seen that by 1953 it was seriously suggested that as a temporary expedient the line be extended to Fulham and Wimbledon along the *Route D* alignment. The complication arose from the need to allow for accommodation of *Route D* and the projection of *Route C* to Croydon instead. All this required the Victoria station design to allow for its temporary use as a terminus, and yet enable the line to be extended both south or south-west, with provision for later adaptation for same-level interchange between the two tube lines. Some concessions to all this were made until all was simplified later. A new ticket hall would be built beneath the main line station forecourt with escalators to the new tube-level island platform, and a separate interchange route would be built to connect with the District Line.

Construction

The construction of an underground railway is inevitably a slow and complex affair. Building the Victoria Line from Victoria to Walthamstow took over six years, in spite of efforts to reduce the construction time. The phasing of the complex work at Oxford Circus was the limiting factor in central London; indeed the reconstruction of this station was not only the last major work to be completed, but it was also the first contract to start following the government go-ahead. Exploratory work beneath the 'circus' itself began on 20th September 1962 in order to establish the exact position of the pipes and mains of the utility services; this had to be known before they could be diverted, and diversion was necessary before any work could begin on the new underground ticket hall. Other difficult parts of the programme included the station works at Victoria, Green Park, Euston and Highbury, the running tunnels between Victoria and Oxford Circus and between Tottenham and Walthamstow, and also the Northern City Line diversion tunnel at Highbury. However, all these works could be pressed ahead quickly as the engineers had had years to finalise many design and construction details.

This August 1963 view from Northumberland Park station shows the bleak landscape upon which the new Victoria Line depot would be built. Alan A Jackson

By the end of 1963 contracts had been placed for over £22million worth of work, including all the shields and tunnel lining. Over 20 working shafts had been sunk and over 30 working sites occupied. At Highbury the diversion tunnel for the northbound Northern City Line was under construction while work had begun outside King's Cross main line station by demolishing property to form a working site. At Euston part of the new ticket hall and escalators to the Northern Line (Charing Cross branch) platforms were nearly complete. A massive steel bridge had been erected across Oxford Circus to allow work to begin there on the new ticket hall. Work had started at Victoria on the District Line interchange passages and the associated lengthening eastwards of the District platforms.

By the autumn of 1964 work was proceeding on all the contracts except those for the three northernmost stations, and the value of the work had reached £25million. By the end of that year 33 shafts had been sunk and 40 working sites were occupied. Running tunnels were being driven from 15 tunnel faces, eight of these using mechanical excavating shields and seven using shields employing hand mining. There were also seven station tunnel shields in use.

Major progress was made during 1965 in pushing ahead the tunnels, with about three-quarters of the running tunnels and over half the station tunnels complete by the year's end. On one tunnelling drive the then world record for soft ground tunnelling was broken with a rate of 470 feet (140m) per week. Ticket halls were complete or well advanced at Seven Sisters, King's Cross, Euston (partly opened in March), Oxford Circus, Green Park and Victoria. Good progress had been made on the escalator shafts and low-level passages at Seven Sisters, Euston, Warren Street, Oxford Circus, Green Park and Victoria. The last three major contracts had been let – for Walthamstow, Blackhorse Road and Tottenham Hale. Extensive work had been undertaken at the Northumberland Park depot site where a temporary track fabrication depot had been built; some tracklaying had begun here and was proceeding into the tunnels towards Seven Sisters station.

The year 1966 saw the completion of all running tunnels (on 20th September) and 23 of the 24 station tunnels. The experimental tunnels north of Finsbury Park were by now integral with the rest of the running tunnels. Although extensive use had been made of the new concrete or flexible iron linings, much of the line had nevertheless utilised traditional bolted iron segments, for example in stations and passageways and where the ground was likely to be unsound (where some use was also made of compressed-air working). In the same year escalator shafts were complete at all but three stations and contracts were placed for substations, cablework and the control room at Euston. Tracklaying proceeded.

The major construction work was substantially wrapped up during 1967. All tunnelling was complete except for a short subway at Oxford Circus. Long-welded rails had been laid throughout, having been brought in by special trains from Northumberland Park depot and laid into the sleeper fastenings that had already been secured in the correct position and concreted in place. When they were no longer needed for access, the working shafts were either filled in or utilised for fan or draught relief purposes. Teams were engaged in fitting out the line and stations. The Euston control room shell was completed and equipping began. Northumberland Park depot substation was commissioned and five of the other eight substations were equipped. The finishing work continued during 1968 when the Victoria Line approached its opening, which was to take place in three stages.

The construction of the line had been very intricate, owing to the warren of existing tunnels and passages through which it had to thread its way, and because of the construction and diversion work required at stations in daily use and around tunnels through which trains still ran. The construction programme had been carefully planned by using a system of network analysis aided by computer – a fairly revolutionary approach at the time. Although many attempts were made to arrest programme slippages, a year was cumulatively lost. Major factors were the time taken to assemble the necessary expertise at the start, and the constant shortage of manpower, especially miners; a boom in the construction industry from 1962 made competition fierce. Ground conditions were sometimes worse than feared, at Oxford Circus nine months were lost in diversions of services, and six months were lost in tunnelling at Euston. The decision to introduce more advanced technology (such as automatic trains) also created delays, especially when deliveries were late anyway. A serious fire at Tottenham Hale introduced further delay and the four stations at the north end of the line were incomplete at the time of opening.

Perhaps surprisingly the Kinnear Moodie 'drum digger' tunnelling machine which had fared so well on the experimental tunnels proved to be slightly less superior to the alternative digging machine, of the centre shaft type, made by McAlpine. A Mark II drum digger was devised but was defeated by bad ground before it could fully demonstrate its capabilities. Some of the engineering involved was quite remarkable and a description of some of the larger works follows.

Diversion of existing railway tunnels was required at Euston (described already) and at Highbury and Finsbury Park. Apart from driving new lengths of tunnel, the work involved the construction of junction tunnels around the existing lines. This was difficult work that involved the excavation of the ground surrounding the old tunnels that had to be accessed from new headings or shafts. As this work proceeded the large-diameter junction tunnel was gradually formed and new tunnel segments erected, the existing tunnel being carefully supported within the new tunnel while this was done. Then the old tunnel-iron was dismantled and the track was temporarily supported until a more permanent trackbed could be laid. Finally, track was installed in the new tunnels and the line diverted.

At Finsbury Park, the ongoing absence of hoped-for BR electrification and the need to economise on capital expenditure meant that the preferred option to release the tube platforms was to cut back the Northern City Line to Drayton Park, which took effect after the last train on 3rd October 1964. A coach service shuttle ran between the two stations until the Victoria Line opened; the traffic day along the whole line was also shortened to operate from about 6.45am to 8pm (these times prevailed until closure in 1975 when the whole line closed for reconstruction upon transfer to British Rail).

Work then began on the 3150ft (960m) diversion of the southbound Piccadilly Line through the former Northern City northbound platform. Once constructed, the route was switched at the northern end simply by commissioning new signalling and changing the (temporary) points. However there was a 5ft (1.5m) difference in level where the old and new routes entered the southern junction tunnel, about 200ft (60m) north of Arsenal station. This required the old line to be supported on a massive trestle. On the day of the change-over the trestle had to be demolished and removed, and the track laid in on the new alignment to connect with that already laid in the diversion tunnel – an intensive task completed by 2pm on Sunday 3rd October 1965, having started at close of traffic on Saturday night.

At Highbury & Islington the northbound Northern City Line was switched through a new platform. To speed up the work on the 2450ft (750m) diversion, the Northern

The former Northern City Line southbound tunnel at Finsbury Park was commandeered for the Victoria Line. This view shows the platform area being reconstructed c.1965.

New tunnelling and alterations to existing tunnelling at Finsbury Park.

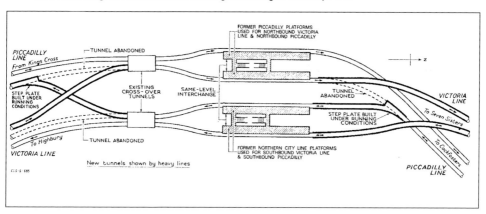

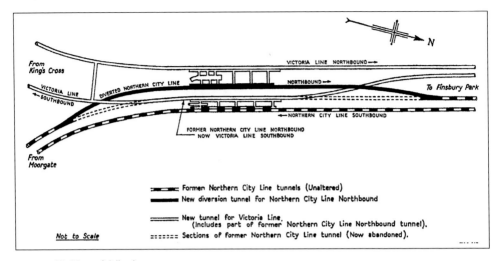

Highbury & Islington.

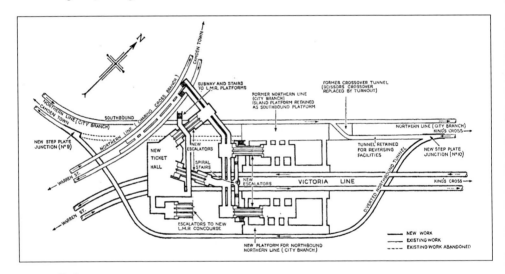

Euston.

City train service was re-arranged after 8pm each night from 11th May 1963 (until mid-evening services were withdrawn in 1964), freeing the northbound tunnel in the Highbury area for the engineers. A single-line shuttle service ran on the southbound line between Finsbury Park and Essex Road, where it connected with another shuttle, on the northbound line, between there and Moorgate. For a brief period tunnel possession was required in the Finsbury Park area when the northern shuttle operated on the northbound line from Finsbury Park to Drayton Park, thence the southbound line as far as Essex Road. The Highbury diversion tunnel and new platform came into use on Sunday 15th August 1965. Work then began to plug the new southbound

Victoria Line into the now-vacant tunnel and to modernise the old platform. There was some uncertainty as to what to do at street level. In the end a so-called 'temporary' station was opened on 7th April 1968 on the site of the former BR station. This was reached by a pair of escalators astride a fixed stairway and connected with what until the previous day had been the lower lift landing. At the top of the escalators was a semi-permanent building that surrounded the lift machine area, but it led into a structure like a very large garden shed whose rear abutted the (permanent) bridge over the North London Line platforms and front hid coyly behind a temporary post office that effortlessly hid the station from view. Thirty-five years later these temporary buildings are still in service, though the ticket hall has been patched up, refurbished and rearranged several times in the interim. It seems the freehold is in the hands of the main line railway and is awaiting a suitable development opportunity. The old station over the road still stands, derelict.

Oxford Circus was the biggest station reconstruction. Essentially, a new ticket hall was constructed beneath the 'circus' with escalators down to an intermediate level and further escalators down to lower concourses. These were built between pairs of Victoria and Bakerloo Line platforms, with which the Victoria Line offered same-level interchange. An escalator also led from the intermediate level to the Central Line. The new construction was to be used mainly for 'Way In' traffic, leaving the existing three Bakerloo Line and two Central Line escalators and the old ticket hall areas available for the 'Way Out' traffic. In addition, a major re-arrangement of low-level passageways was required to ease flows and to replace some passages that would be cut through by the new running tunnels. The old subways were replaced in a carefully phased programme, the station having to remain fully operational throughout. Some of the construction took place in waterlogged ground and chemical consolidation was needed.

It had been decided to bridge the entire road surface of the 'circus' with a massive steel deck, popularly known as the Oxford Circus Umbrella, to facilitate the construction of the new ticket hall. The 600 tons (610t) of prefabricated steel sections were erected during the August Bank Holiday weekend of 1963, the 'circus' and some surrounding streets being closed from early afternoon on Saturday 3rd August until 6:30am on Tuesday 6th August. This decking initially had an area of 2500 sq yds (2090 sq m), including the ramps that took the traffic up to deck level, 3ft 6ins (1.07m) above the road surface. The deck sections were mounted on a steel framework which itself sat on some 25 concrete cylinders, which had been sunk through the road surface previously. The temporary arrangements allowed traffic to flow westbound along Oxford Street and southbound along Regent Street, the return flows using other roads.

The 'umbrella' was extended about 100ft (30m) eastwards along Oxford Street during the 1966 August Bank Holiday to allow construction of the subway linking the existing ticket hall to the new one, the working period being similar to that of 1963. Its task complete, the 'umbrella' was removed during the Easter holiday weekend of 1968, the area being closed off from 11:30pm on Thursday 11th April until the very early morning on Tuesday 16th April.

During the time the deckwork was in position the new ticket hall area and upper escalators were excavated and public utility services re-routed, many of the materials required being delivered to the working site at night through holes created by removing decking panels. In due course the new ticket hall roof, which was to support the roadway above, was completed and the load of the 'umbrella' bridge was gradually transferred from the special columns to the permanent roadway.

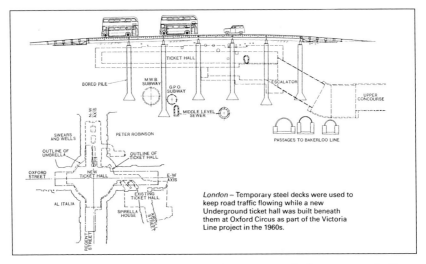

Within the diagram:
TICKET HALL
M.W.B. SUBWAY
BORED PILE
G.P.O. SUBWAY
ESCALATOR
UPPER CONCOURSE
MIDDLE LEVEL SEWER
N-W AXIS
SWEARS AND WELLS
PETER ROBINSON
PASSAGES TO BAKERLOO LINE
OUTLINE OF UMBRELLA
OUTLINE OF TICKET HALL
OXFORD STREET
NEW TICKET HALL
E-W AXIS
EXISTING TICKET HALL
AL ITALIA
SPIRELLA HOUSE
REGENT STREET

London – Temporary steel decks were used to keep road traffic flowing while a new Underground ticket hall was built beneath them at Oxford Circus as part of the Victoria Line project in the 1960s.

Section through the new ticket hall at Oxford Circus showing the temporary umbrella bridge. The complications of existing underground passages may be seen.

Another difficult part of the work at Oxford Circus arose from the construction of the southbound Victoria Line station tunnel. The new tunnel was required to pass just beneath the third basement level of the Peter Robinson department store and it was necessary to spread some of the load of the building before tunnelling began. From the working shaft at Cavendish Square, a 250yds (230m) access tunnel was driven to a point beneath the store. A pre-stressed concrete raft was then constructed below the basement to spread the load. The lower side of the raft was formed of weak concrete and intersected the line of the future southbound tunnel roof. The crown of the station tunnel was eventually driven through the bottom of the raft, and as each of the specially reinforced steel tunnel rings was completed it assumed some of the load of the building.

Just north of Victoria station the running tunnels passed beneath the site of the former Watney brewery, which had deep foundation piles. To speed up the work on the northbound tunnel drive, the drum digger was fitted with hardened cutting teeth that allowed it to chew its way slowly through the concrete piles as they were encountered, though this did put a strain on the equipment.

At Victoria itself, the main line station had been built on the back-filled site of the former Grosvenor Canal basin, which was originally a reservoir for the Chelsea Waterworks Company and then adapted to take water-borne freight. Chemical treatment was needed to consolidate both this ground and adjacent water-bearing sand and gravel before the Victoria Line tunnels could be constructed. During sewer diversion work part of the former canal basin walls were encountered.

To allow part of the train service to begin at the south end of the line each day, four sidings were to be built south of the station, the outer two capable of being converted into running lines at some future date (because this was a feature actually needed for the Brixton extension the outer sidings were built but not used as such). One of the centre two sidings was built with a larger diameter tunnel and a pit to allow emergency maintenance to be performed.

A view looking west along Oxford Street showing the 'umbrella' being dismantled and exposing the roof of the new ticket hall beneath. Kinnear Moodie

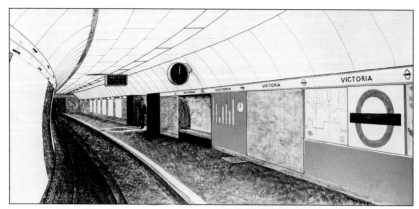

Varying proposals for platform finishes at the new stations. LT Museum

TOM SMITH

The great Victoria Line muddle

THE ONLY visible signs of London's new underground railway, the Victoria Line, are sinister growths like that steamship tower at Green Park, and the vast turtle shell over Oxford Circus. Exactly what is going on under Londoners' feet, and how is the project, billed to cost £56 million and take six years, getting along?

"More like £75 million, at the least," said our Victoria Line man when we asked him, "and at least two extra years."

For instance, they've already managed to immobilise two digger shields—the great machines worth £17,000 that do the tunnelling. They are the most modern tunnelling equipment ever used, eating their way through at a rate of 36 feet a day.

Clay-eaters

The trouble is, they are designed for a diet of clay. So when two of them ran into waterlogged gravel, the whole tunnel caved in around them. Now one of them is sitting, swamped, somewhere under Green Park, and another is under a reservoir in North London.

A thorough preliminary survey would have avoided trouble. But preliminary surveys are expensive and take a long time.

"*Contracts worth £17,500,000*

already placed," *boasted London Transport in 1963.*

Unfortunately, they sometimes placed the contracts a bit too quickly. There were crisis situations when the planning people had to take snap decisions because they could almost hear the rumble of tunnellers catching up with them. It costs an awful lot to stop the tunnelling operation.

Lavish brick

The planners weren't helped by the time it took to get decisions out of London Transport. Somehow letters and plans seemed to get lost for weeks somewhere between the Permanent Way department and its rival, the New Works department.

Technical limitations of firms involved were pretty expensive, too. The engineers originally designed the new booking-hall at Oxford Circus in lavish brick. When they discovered it took no less than three months to order bricks they switched to concrete. But not the cheap, pre-stressed kind—that needs quite complicated mathematics. They used old-fashioned, expensive mass concrete.

"*Progress 'all along the line,'*" *boasted London Transport in 1964.*

But the worst trouble, the one that really delays things, is the labour problem. There is a great

shortage of the skilled and semi-skilled people needed. At the moment skilled men are leaving one job when it gets difficult and signing on with another contractor for an easier stretch of the line.

And until you solve the labour problem, and get the job running smoothly, nothing can really go ahead. London Transport keep on about their modern techniques, their critical path programming and network analysis, but they are not much use without an adequate labour force. Whatever the findings, the contractors will take their own time.

"*Computer to be used to programme and co-ordinate work,*" *boasted London Transport in 1963.*

How did they ever imagine they'd get by on a mere £56 million? "Oh," said our man, "Government outfits tend to give out the minimum figure, the amount things would cost for a modern industrial structure if everything went absolutely perfectly."

Not everybody was quite as complimentary as LT's relentless press machine would have preferred.

Several different possible finishes for Victoria Line stations were mocked up on a disused platform at Aldwych to see what they looked like at full scale. LT Museum

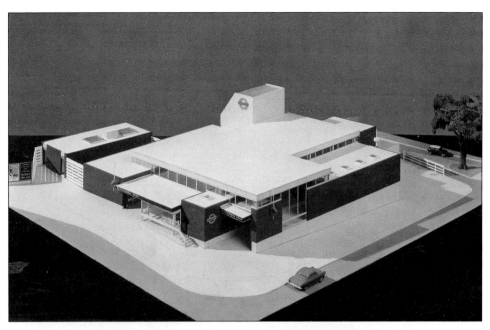

Blackhorse Road was to be the only station with an independent surface building. A model of the station was built in order to gauge overall appearance. LT Museum

This view shows the depot at Northumberland Park under construction. On the extreme left the rail connection with the main line may be seen; this was removed later. A. A. Jackson

New Features

Detailed plans for equipping the tube tunnels and stations had begun in the 1950s. During the early years the Victoria Line was not intended to differ in any material way from other Underground lines, other than by having all the latest trains and equipment. By the time of authorisation, however, widespread automation was favoured to reduce the need for large numbers of additional staff that were becoming difficult to recruit and were absorbing an increasing share of the traffic receipts. Four new developments were adopted for the Victoria Line: automatic ticket issuing and checking, stations run from a single 'operations room', automatic routeing of trains supervised from a central control room and automatically driven trains.

With automatic trains mooted, it was desired to abolish doors directly from cab to platform. In an attempt to retain urgent access double front doors were considered a possible option (resulting in central 'driver's' position), as this 1963 photo of a mock up shows. This presented all sorts of other complications and was not pursued.

London Transport had sold a large volume of tickets from automatic ticket machines for many years, and for the Victoria Line it was desired both to increase this proportion and to devise a method of checking the tickets automatically in electronic barriers, rather than by traditional manual checks. In doing this, LT worked closely with the Advanced Data Corporation, an American company that was developing similar equipment. Initial experiments took place in 1963 with a selection of different types of encoding possibilities, some of which were tried on tickets to see how they withstood handling. The following year an experimental barrier entered service for 'Way In' passengers at Stamford Brook station, which used specially printed tickets. Further barriers were tried subsequently at Ravenscourt Park, Chiswick Park and Acton Town, using a variety of special tickets and encoding techniques. As a result of these experiments a workable design of barrier evolved, using a system of card tickets backed with an iron oxide coating that could be encoded magnetically. The faces of the new tickets were coloured yellow to distinguish them for the benefit of passengers and staff from the then existing range, which could only be checked manually.

To test the concept realistically it was decided to have a full-scale trial at Hammersmith (District & Piccadilly) station in 1966. A new ticket office was constructed centrally in the main ticket hall and 14 free-standing automatic ticket machines were also provided. All could issue the new tickets and the ticket office could also issue encoded season tickets. On one wall of the ticket office a large self-service 'Multi-fare' machine issued several types of ticket to any Underground station; there was also a note-changing machine designed to handle ten-shilling (50p) and one-pound notes. A feature of these two machines was that the booking clerks could service them from within the office. Six automatic gates were provided for passengers holding yellow tickets, three for 'Way In' traffic and three for 'Way Out'. The manned barriers were retained because of the need to accommodate non-encoded tickets issued by other stations. The ticket collector no longer dealt with excess fares owed by passengers, who were directed to a separate ticket office window within the barrier line, which issued encoded excess fare tickets for use in the automatic gates.

The experiment was deemed very successful and it was decided to introduce automatic ticket issuing and checking on the Victoria Line as a prelude to systemwide introduction. Since this authority was received only in May 1967, after much of the ticket hall construction had already been completed, some delay was inevitable as alterations were made to ticket hall areas to accommodate the new equipment and revised passenger flows, but the changes were all achieved within the existing box structures. Not all the installations were complete even when the line had reached Victoria, and initially a greater reliance was placed on traditional manual ticket inspection than had been planned. However, within a year all tickets issued between or from Victoria Line stations had the capability of operating automatic gates.

The operations room philosophy presumed that the station supervisor might be used to greater effect if he (there were no female inspectors or station managers then) resided in purpose-built accommodation with efficient communication facilities; these would include closed-circuit television monitoring of the rest of the station, direct line telephone links to all key points and public address facilities to all areas of the station.

A full-scale experiment was therefore conducted at Holborn station, starting in December 1962. The operations room was constructed high above the concourse at the bottom of the four main escalators, an excellent vantage point. The station supervisor viewed the busy scene below through 'one-way' mirrored windows. Each of the four main platforms was equipped with at least one television camera monitored from the operations room, which was also given controls to turn, tilt and focus most of the cameras. Full public address facilities were given, and a new feature was the introduction of 'Passenger Information Points' on the platforms – an intercom system allowing passengers wanting information to speak to the supervisor (Russell Square platforms were later added to the system). Also considered successful, operations rooms were incorporated into the Victoria Line planning process.

The signalling system on the Underground had been largely automatic since just after the turn of the century, except, of course, at junctions and reversing points where signal cabins remained necessary. But even here the tendency had been to build new signal cabins to cover increasingly larger areas, often at the cost of closing several smaller cabins. In the late 1950s experiments had taken place on the Northern Line to automate some of the cabins in the central area by replacing the signalmen with programme machines. These machines incorporated a long plastic strip containing punched holes that represented train movements through the relevant junctions. As each train passed through the junction the strip, mounted between rollers, moved along (or stepped) to the next row of holes. The coded commands produced by the machines were then used to operate the levers on the signal frame itself.

To supervise the action of these machines a small control room was built at Leicester Square incorporating an illuminated track diagram of the central area of the Northern Line, together with push button controls to adjust the working of the programme machines in the event of trains running out of sequence, or to operate the points and signals by remote control. It was decided to install a similar system on the entire Victoria Line, supervised from a purpose-built control room at Euston. In theory one (or sometimes two) 'regulators' on duty at a time would replace perhaps four or five signalmen. By putting the controller in the same room it was also considered that communication would be much improved.

Automatically driven trains had long been a quest of railway operators, in particular as a way of preventing trains overrunning signals at danger. Automation also suggested that the crew could be reduced from two to one per train, an attractive goal on a new railway, especially at a difficult time for recruitment. London Transport's particular desire for automatic operation was boosted by the peculiar circumstances of deep-level tube operation in single-track tunnels: in the unusual event of the train driver becoming incapacitated it was expected that the guard (who was trained to drive) would get the train to the next station. If, however, there was no guard then some other means of extricating the train quickly had to be devised – automation appeared to meet this need.

There was discussion about having entirely unmanned trains (the Chief Signal Engineer's aspiration) but the problems of addressing failures promptly were intractable and there was in any case doubt about whether the public or railway inspectorate would accept such operation.

After initial experimentation some of the proposed equipment was installed on a track between South Ealing and Acton Town, which, during the day, was reserved for the operation of test trains; a District Line car was fitted with the trial train-borne equipment. The results were promising, so the next stage was to transfer the trackside equipment to a stretch of line between Stamford Brook and Ravenscourt Park. A District Line driving car was fitted with prototype train-borne equipment and trials began in passenger service in April 1963. The special car was placed at the east end of a District Line passenger train that operated normally for the majority of the time. However, when the train arrived at Stamford Brook (eastbound) the driver selected automatic operation and the train proceeded all the way to Ravenscourt Park without the need for the driver to touch anything, stopping and starting at any intermediate red signals as required. This experiment, too, was deemed very successful.

Following the results of this small-scale experiment it was then decided to engage in a much larger trial. The Central Line branch between Woodford and Hainault was at that time mainly operated as an independent shuttle service. The Central Line was also blessed with three experimental 0-car trains (classed as 1960 stock) which were non-standard with the fleet then in course of delivery. The whole of the Woodford-Hainault section of line was equipped with facilities for automatic train operation, and the prototype trains converted into five 4-car automatic trains. Equipping was completed during April 1964, and the automatic trains were then tested.

The prototype equipment used on the Hainault shuttle service did suggest a number of relatively minor improvements, but on the whole it performed most satisfactorily and the decision was made to equip the Victoria Line for the operation of fully automatic trains. As installed, the Victoria Line signalling system therefore differed radically from that used elsewhere in the British Isles. Automatic operation relied on sequences of auto-drive commands being transmitted from 'spots' on the track, with the running of the train at all times being governed by one of three safety codes which had to be continuously received by the train; both the commands and safety codes were received by pick-up coils mounted on the train's leading bogie. With most of the 'signals' effectively replaced by electronic codes only a very few conventional signals were installed, mainly for use by ballast trains and in emergency manual working, and for the benefit of station staff.

There were many thoughts about the train design. In the early 1950s it was proposed to use a new train (the 1952 stock) then on the drawing board. As the years rolled by the proposed design of the moment emulated the latest design on other lines. Towards the end of the decade some thought went into the use of articulated trains, where bogies were shared between adjacent cars. The advantage was that this increased the flexibility in locating the doors, to help reduce train boarding times. Trains of all-motored, regenerative-braked, fairly short cars were contemplated, with 10-car trains (of two 5-car units). However the design relied on the very shallow curves on the Victoria Line and it would have been difficult to get the trains to Acton Works for overhaul over Piccadilly Line tracks. When the Victoria Line nominal tunnel size was finally set at 12ft (3.7m) it became hard to devise an articulated carbody structure giving a sufficient distance between bogie centres to give a satisfactory train layout and it was simpler to retain the traditional 8-car train formation.

The main starting point was therefore the 1960 prototype stock, which already indicated the direction of the prevailing thinking. The 1960 stock adopted several new features, chief among which were a new body profile and much larger, double-glazed windows. The 8-car trains were made up of two 4-car units, each consisting of two motor cars (with driving cabs) and a pair of intermediate trailers. Each motor car was fitted with four traction motors (instead of two as hitherto) with pairs of motors connected in permanent series, another new feature. These principles formed the foundation of the Victoria Line trains. By late 1963 or early 1964 the new design was still based on the 1960 stock underframe but with a restyled body incorporating a number of new features and which could accommodate automatic operation. Models and mock-ups were built and studied, and these appear to have been heavily influenced by the design consultants. Within the next year several fundamental changes had been made, including a re-profiled body and less 'angular' interior fittings.

This 1965 mock up shows a further attempt to deal with rapid access to and from the cab by means of a small platform outside the front door and a handrail so that the driver could ease himself across to the platform, or vice versa. In this view the cab droplight can be seen in lieu of a side door.

Above **This model car (the design having probably benefited from the attention of Design Research Unit) shows a tidying up of the front but with improved handrails and 'step plate' designs. DRU attempted to maximise window heights to improve ambience and platform visibility but in the end the 1960 stock pattern was retained and door windows increased in height instead.**

Left **This mock up of a car interior shows radical new design input. In the event the design was to revert very much more closely to the 1960 stock.**

47

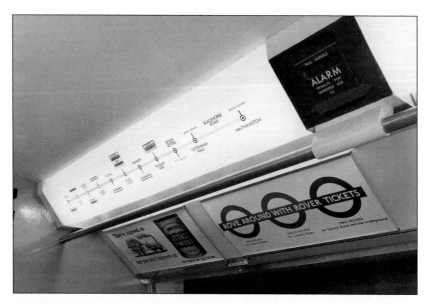

DRU was very keen on interior illuminated maps to improve presence. This view shows map and other detail, including a proposed pull down ventilator. LT has never pursued back-illuminated maps, and attempts to use lamp enclosures of this sort have always resulted in maintenance and cleaning complications. LT Museum

The proposed cab layout is a radical improvement on anything before. The right hand main operator's position (with door controls prominent) follows from most platforms being on the right hand side. In the event, a left hand driving position was finally adopted (possibly for signal sighting reasons when stock was operating on other lines). LT Museum

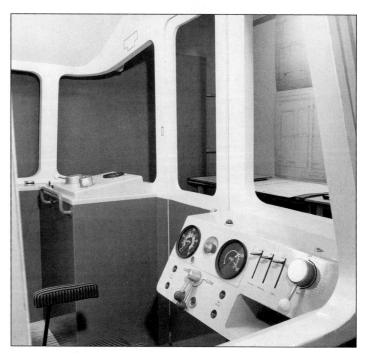

This mock up shows the design in its near final form. Subsequent adjustments included removal of the two whistle shrouds (over the headlights) when the whistles were incorporated into the front grabrails. The destination indicator and front vent were also remodelled. LT Museum

The 30½ trains that were built for the Victoria Line were of 8-cars, divided into two identical 4-car units. The cars at the ends of each unit were motor cars, each equipped with a driving cab at the outer end. The cab design had given some cause for concern. Conventional cabs had doors at each side (to allow drivers to get in and out, mainly at stations), a door into the passenger compartment, and an end door to allow access between units or (if at the end of a train) access to and from the track for emergency use. The concern was that if 'auto driving' had been selected a driver might be tempted to open the side door for some reason and get out, or fall out, with the train moving or about to move; this was (however implausible) not entirely unknown even on a conventional train where the driver was supposed to be anchored to his control handle while the train was moving. Furthermore, on a one-person train it was essential that the driver be able to look out safely at stations, and an opening window was called for (not technically easy if a side door were fitted). For these reasons it was decided to avoid side doors. However it was still considered helpful for a driver to be able to get on and off the train at a platform if the circumstances warranted it. An early idea was to provide duplicate front doors at either side of the cab (requiring a central control position) so a driver could clamber out onto a platform if needed but this presented so many other operational objections it was unsupportable. In the end side doors were jettisoned. This had the result that if the operator had to get out of a very crowded train – where progress through the cars was impossible – he had to swing himself across the front of the train in a practical though somewhat undignified manner. The 1960 stock ATO conversions had the side doors removed and opening droplights fitted that were interlocked with the traction circuits to prevent the train moving with either window open, and this was the system adopted on the Victoria Line trains too.

The cab controls were laid out primarily with automatic operation in mind, but a combined driving and braking controller was provided for emergency and shunting use. Two buttons were provided in order to start the train, and these were duplicated on each side of the cab. The trains were not designed to be uncoupled under service conditions, which was once the practice on the Underground but had largely ceased in the previous decade (in 1959 it had been the intention to run thirty 8-car trains per hour in the peaks and twenty 4-car trains per hour off-peak). For this reason the LT-standard 'Wedgelock' couplers were not fully automatic as on earlier stocks but were fitted with manual coupler switches, a by-product of which was that they were very reliable. The two intermediate cars of each 4-car unit were to be trailers and presented no particular challenges. A new feature common to all cars in each unit was a public address system, which had also been tested on the 1960 stock.

Technically the trains were not so very different from the 1960 stock but one significant feature was the addition of rheostatic braking. By this means a call for brakes connected the traction motors across a rheostat (a set of resistances); the motors acted as generators and the train's energy was burnt off as heat in the resistances. If additional braking was required air brakes were applied to the trailer wheels and, if necessary the motor wheels as well. The advantage of this system was a significant reduction of brake block dust and brake maintenance. Earlier plans for trains to 'regenerate' braking current and return it to the traction system (instead of burning it off) were abandoned as too difficult – it had been tried in the 1930s without much practical success and despite further experiments during 1957–8 the problems were insuperable: even in the twenty-first century regenerative braking continues to challenge ingenuity. Three manufacturer's regenerative brake equipment had been tested on a 1936 stock unit and in the end the British Thomson-Houston equipment was rebuilt for tests of regenerative braking on a 1960 stock unit; this eventually led to a satisfactory design for Victoria Line use.

The new trains began to be delivered to LT at its West Ruislip depot from September 1967, and after final equipping and initial testing each of the units was transferred to Hainault depot for trials in passenger service on the Woodford–Hainault shuttle, operating automatically. The first trains were then hauled by battery locomotive from Hainault to Northumberland Park depot via Leyton and British Rail tracks, a temporary rail link between the depot and the adjacent Eastern Region lines (initially used for delivery of materials) being used. The link was later removed, allowing the flood prevention wall around the depot to be completed; this was required because the depot site was below the flood level of the nearby River Lea (and the adjacent Eastern Region lines had been engulfed in a flood in 1947). Later Victoria Line trains were delivered via a link with the Piccadilly Line at Finsbury Park.

As the Victoria Line would have a few trains beyond service requirements for a while there was a short-lived proposal during 1969 to use them in 4-car formations on the Northern City Line to replace temporarily 1938 stock of which there was a shortage. In the end it became clear the complexity and cost far outweighed the benefits and it wasn't pursued although quite a lot of work had gone into the proposal.

During the construction period prices had inevitably risen, and the 1962 estimate of £56.1million had increased by £6.8million during the 6½ years taken to build the line. Additional money had also been made available to cover various items not originally allowed for, such as automatic fare collection, automatic trains and other sundry items, which amounted to £3.5million. A roughly similar amount was also put aside for contingencies.

This view of a driver's cab shows the combined traction/brake controller. For technical reasons it had to be on the left hand side and used 'left handed'. The large button on the driver's desk is the 'vigilance' button and has to be kept depressed when the train is being driven manually and off code.
LT Museum

It had originally been assumed that LT would have to start paying interest out of its revenue not long after construction started – rising to several million pounds a year. In March 1964 the Minister authorised interest to be 'capitalised' (that is, added to the total government advance) at least until 1967. The effect was that interest enough to warrant a fares increase would not be charged during the line's construction when, it was argued, passengers were actually getting a worse service because of the disruption. However it did add £5.3million to the £70million cost of the line, which would increase interest charges when it did open. A 'modest' increase in fares was therefore forecast. Some wry observations were made that the passengers benefiting most from the new line would be those making substantially shorter journeys as a result. The charge-by-distance fares system then in force implied that these people would therefore pay less than hitherto, while non-Victoria Line users paid more. Transport funding has rarely claimed to be fair.

Opening

It had been the intention, in 1962, to open the Victoria Line in stages, with Stage 1 opening on 1st September 1967, and the remaining two stages opening at 3-monthly intervals. The phased opening principle still held good after programme slippage. Among the many reasons, it made sense to start earning revenue as soon as possible, it re-opened a rail link between Finsbury Park and Highbury & Islington, it allowed the relatively lightly used northern section of the line to test the new equipment under operational conditions, and it allowed many of the new staff to train and acclimatise to the new line before it became really busy.

The first section of line to open was therefore the Walthamstow to Highbury section, which began without ceremony at start of traffic on Sunday 1st September 1968, exactly a year behind programme (the timetable had been operated, without passengers, from 26th August, only three weeks after this section had been handed over by the engineers, so the period for training was very limited). Shortly before opening, Walthamstow Hoe Street station was renamed Walthamstow Central. At first a 4-minute service operated in the rush hours; trains reversed in the southbound platform at Highbury during the morning peak, and the northbound in the evening, to provide the best connections for City workers using the Northern City Line. All trains ran to Walthamstow during the peak hours with a proportion turned back at Seven Sisters during the off-peak. There were some anxious times just before opening as the tunnels were cool and extremely damp, which was affecting the signalling; frantic efforts were made to dry them out, but once a service began things eventually dried out of their own accord (with cooling rather than warming now the problem). In fact none of the stations was quite finished and contractors were still on site; the arrangements at Walthamstow were makeshift to say the least. A feature of the three northern stations was the provision of automatically operated car parks and these quickly proved popular.

Blackhorse Road station on opening day with builders still in residence.
Capital Transport

On opening day many facilities were far from complete as this view of the bus interchange at Walthamstow shows. Capital Transport

Although a new joint ticket office was built at Walthamstow it wasn't ready on opening day and passengers had to use the old Great Eastern Railway building, with not much clue that it was the way in to a new state of the art Underground line. Capital Transport

Blackhorse Road ticket hall shortly after opening. The centrally positioned ticket office has a ticket window on each side and an excess fare window within the barrier line. The automatic exit barriers are on the left, with Way In barriers on the right (the exit barrier next to the ticket office is reversible). LT Museum

On Saturday 7th September there were widespread alterations to bus routes in London as part of the first stage of the much-heralded Bus Reshaping Plan. In Walthamstow a system of feeder services was created to operate into the new (but not quite complete) bus station, built to provide good interchange with the new Victoria Line. Another system of feeder buses served Finsbury Park station, and various changes were also made to a number of trunk routes. Through (bus-rail) tickets were never provided – intriguingly transport integrator London Transport stopped most examples of such things before the Second World War – but flat fares were available at sixpence (2½p) a go which was comparatively quick with the new one-person operated buses.

The next section of railway, to Warren Street, opened three months later on 1st December, again without ceremony (timetabled running of empty trains had begun on 25th November). This time trains reversed in the new southbound platform there, and at this stage the northbound platform was not used. The service pattern and intervals remained similar to those prevailing under Stage 1. On reaching Warren Street, the scissors crossover at Highbury was simplified, and became a trailing emergency crossover; there was only ever a trailing crossover at Warren Street.

This view shows part of a gleaming new train at Walthamstow on the opening day. The shiny finish lasted a few years but eventually became dull and grey. Capital Transport

The cross-central London link to Oxford Circus, Green Park and Victoria, and the official opening of the new line, came on 7th March 1969 (timetabled trial running having begun on 24th February). From this point onwards the Victoria Line became a very busy railway. By May/June 1970 the busiest section, between Victoria and Green Park, was carrying 15,000 passengers in one direction during the peak evening hour. This compares well with the 1955 estimate of 14,000. The annual traffic in passenger miles carried on the new line was estimated as 229 million. The initial train service over the section from Victoria to Seven Sisters was 2–2½ minutes during the peak, half the service being projected on to Walthamstow. Off peak a proportion of trains from Victoria also reversed at King's Cross as for some years the traffic demand further north was much less than in recent years. At Victoria all trains usually reversed alternately in each platform. A further stage of bus reshaping, along the Seven Sisters Road and through the West End, took place on 24th January 1970 after new travelling patterns had settled down; the emphasis was on encouraging passengers to switch to the new tube.

The Chairman, Mr. Maurice Holmes,
and the Members of the London Transport Board
request the pleasure of the company of

A. B. Beaumont Esq.
at the opening of

THE VICTORIA LINE

BY

HER MAJESTY THE QUEEN
at Green Park Station at 11 00 on Friday 7 March 1969

R.S.V.P. To The Chief Public Relations Officer
55 Broadway, London S.W.1

Dress
Lounge Suit

An outline of the programme is shown on the back
Full details and a ticket of admission will be sent on receipt of your acceptance

Above **H.M. Queen Elizabeth II at the opening of the Victoria Line. To show how things worked she was provided with a sixpenny piece with which to buy a ticket and use the automatic barriers.**

Left **Light Blue Royal Opening Invitation**

Interior of new 1967 stock car shortly after delivery. LT Museum

The public found the beginnings of what then was regarded as the most modern urban railway in the world: smart, quite spacious ticket halls, gleaming escalators with their brushed metallic finishes, platforms tiled in two-tone blue/grey with bright metallic trim and coloured motifs (different at each station) along the platform seat recesses, and smart new automatically driven trains. The styling was heavily influenced by LT's own design panel and the work of their external consultants, Design Research Unit. Many of the new features had previously been shown to the public at an exhibition at The Design Centre, in London, in 1967. Not quite all were happy and there was some dissent in the newspapers about the 'late lavatorial' style, relieved only by 'austere' decorated tiles, and the only true stimulation likely to result from the commercial advertising – the 'poor man's art gallery'.

While all the stations were broadly similar in design there were detail changes. Between Victoria and King's Cross the station name 'bulls-eyes' were on internally illuminated glass panels, while at other stations they were in the usual enamelled form but floodlit. At most stations the ceiling was finished in white melamine sheeting which distributed the fluorescent light evenly over the platforms. North of Seven Sisters a more economical roof finish was applied where the tunnel segments were simply painted black and the illumination installed in a wide white trough to reflect the light downwards.

Power for the new line was supplied from nine new substations, at Forest Road, Seven Sisters, Manor House, Drayton Park, Cloudesley Road, Cobourg Street (also a power switching centre), Dover Street, Gillingham Street and at the depot at Northumberland Park. Each was remotely supervised from a control room at Manor House. The high-tension supply was obtained from the Underground's main generating station at Lots Road, which was re-equipped with higher capacity plant to take on the additional load (the power station at Greenwich was modernised at about the same time, primarily to assist during periods of peak load). Unlike the rest of the Underground, power cables supplied a high voltage supply to each station and local transformers converted it to lower voltage to supply local equipment.

The signalling control (or 'regulating') room at Euston was available shortly before the first stage of the line opened, and was designed to accommodate both the Victoria Line as built and its southwards extension to Brixton, about which more below. It also had provision for controlling the signalling on the Northern Line, whose controls were transferred from other sites a few years later. The signalling and pointwork at Walthamstow, Seven Sisters, Northumberland Park depot outlet, King's Cross and Victoria were normally under the control of local programme machines which set up the routes required through electro-mechanical 'interlocking machines', which retained the element of mechanical interlocking of signals and points which would otherwise be found in conventional signal boxes. The programme machine control could be over-ridden if necessary either by the train regulator or by the new train-generated destination apparatus (called 'Identra'). Crossovers also existed at Highbury and Warren Street; at these sites the signalling was normally operated automatically for through running, although the regulator could set up other routes as required and automatic train-reversing facilities were also available.

Top right **Victoria was typical of the finish applied to stations south of Seven Sisters.** LT Museum

Right **This view of Walthamstow Central is typical of the stations north of Seven Sisters when new.** LT Museum

59

by Julia Black
An adaptation of a William Morris design. He was born and worked for a time in Walthamstow where a museum displays examples of his work.

by Hans Unger
The black horse also appears as a sculpture, by David McFall, on the exterior of the station.

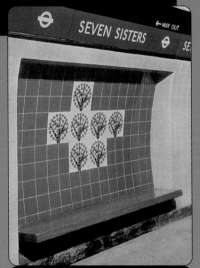

by Edward Bawden
The name is derived from a ferry over the river Lea in earlier times. The word 'hale' is said to be a corruption of 'haul'; or perhaps 'hail'.

by Hans Unger
The seven sisters were seven trees which gave a name to the locality.

by Tom Eckersley
The crossed pistols refer to the
duelling that took place here
when this was outside the edge
of London.

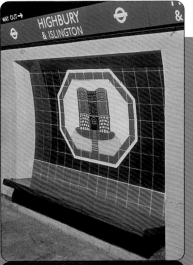

by Edward Bawden
The high bury, manor or castle,
was destroyed at the time of the
Peasants' Revolt (1381).

by Tom Eckersley
A literal design based on a cross
and crowns. The King concerned
(if there ever was one) is not
identified.

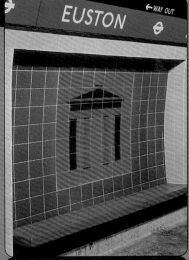

by Tom Eckersley
A reminder of the Doric Arch
which stood on the station site.

by *Crosby/Fletcher/Forbes*
A maze or Warren as a pun on the name. A solution is possible for the traveller with time to spare.

by *Hans Unger*
A device to incorporate the circle of the circus with the linking of the Bakerloo, Central and Victoria Lines.

by *Hans Unger*
A bird's eye view of the trees in the park against the green background of the grass.

by *Edward Bawden*
The great Queen herself, from a silhouette by Benjamin Pearce. A plaque in the ticket hall records the visit of Queen Elizabeth to open the Victoria Line in March 1969.

Communications were considered important on the new line and a major advance was made with the Carrier-Wave system which put trains in constant touch with the control room, even while moving (on other lines trains then had to stop before contact could be made). As the train operator was now the only member of staff on each train, arrangements were made to allow him to get help easily. In addition to Carrier-Wave communication, a special 'Calling-On' light was provided at the back of each train that the operator could activate from the front cab; this authorised the following train to move up to the calling train to render assistance. A short-wave inter-train radio was also provided for use under these circumstances. A feature at platform level was the provision on each platform of three emergency plungers, the operation of which interacted with the automatic train driving circuitry to stop any train in the immediate area; trains could also be stopped from station operations rooms. Another facility on in-town platforms were the Passenger Information Points to the station operations room, following the Holborn experiment. All platforms were provided with full public address equipment, operable from the control room or locally from special positions that had a fold-down step to allow staff to see over the heads of passengers.

The depot was provided with three workshop roads and nine roads with maintenance pits, allowing minor repairs to be performed. Eleven double-length stabling roads were also provided, all of which were under cover. Because of the distance from the main Victoria Line the depot was, and still is, unusual in having a scheduled train service to and from Seven Sisters for staff access, and a short platform (resited more than once) is situated in the depot for this purpose.

This early view of the Cobourg Street control room shows the Victoria Line operation being 'run' by just two people. The Victoria Line controller is at the further of the two upper desks (the nearer one is for the Northern Line), while the service 'regulator' is at the lower desk. The lower diagram shows the position of all trains and the upper one shows the state of the various programme machines. LT Museum

Brixton Extension

Having explained how a working railway was produced from the point when the Act of Parliament of 1955 crystallised the northern section, it is now necessary to see what befell the proposed section south of Victoria. As mentioned earlier the 1955 Act had authorised an alignment that allowed a choice of extension south-westwards towards Fulham or south towards Stockwell, the former possible routeing being preferred. LT-sponsored studies took place that resulted in a detailed report in 1958 that reviewed possible routeings carefully; comparisons were made with a possible extension of the Bakerloo south of Elephant & Castle, for which powers already existed. The report presumed (correctly) that extension of both lines could not be afforded.

The studies concluded that a Victoria Line extension to Fulham and Wimbledon would neither be very good value for money, nor significantly improve public transport facilities. On the other hand an extension to Croydon would also be poor value because construction would be expensive and traffic south of Streatham would be comparatively light. Extension only as far as Streatham, or, better still, Brixton, would be worthwhile and achieve a useful relief of traffic on the Northern Line. Any Victoria Line extension was felt more valuable than Bakerloo extension to Camberwell, but the report noted that if the BTC felt committed to Camberwell then that line should be extended further (to Brixton) in lieu of the Victoria Line. The report was accepted as the basis of future tube planning for south London, with the Victoria Line extension to Brixton (or Streatham) the preferred option.

An early manifestation of the revised thinking appeared in the British Transport Commission Act 1960, which authorised the sidings beyond the platforms at Victoria to be re-aligned (the original termination was under the main line station at Elizabeth Street bridge, the new point was by the junction of Belgrave Road and Gillingham Street). The station would have two platforms, but the tracks were now to continue in a gradual curve to the south, to lead into four sidings the outer two of which were arranged to allow for conversion into future running lines. At the southern end of the platforms escalators would lead into a new ticket hall beneath the Southern Region station forecourt, while farther back along the platforms additional escalators would lead to a concourse beneath the District Line tracks, from which interchange passages would emerge. Any pretensions to be able to accommodate the now defunct *Route D* were abandoned.

By 1963 the Victoria Line had been authorised and London Transport was freed of control by the impoverished British Transport Commission. However, under the 1962 Transport Act both British Railways and London Transport were required to provide properly co-ordinated transport services in London. To fulfil this statutory obligation a joint planning committee was soon established – the Passenger Transport Planning Committee for London. An early decision was made that the Victoria Line ought to be extended at least as far as Brixton, with intermediate stations at Vauxhall and Stockwell. The alignment to Fulham was again considered but the line could not serve Fulham as well as Brixton and the former was officially abandoned for Victoria Line purposes.

The Committee's view was officially expressed in their (unpublished) report of 1965 – 'A Railway Plan for London'. They noted the earlier proposal for a line from Victoria to Croydon, and that this had to be ruled out because of the enormous cost and the expected stagnation of inner-suburban traffic. But they felt that sufficient justification still existed for a limited extension to Brixton only, about 3½ miles (5.6km). Much of the justification rested on the new interchange facilities that would be opened up with the Southern Region and the buses at Brixton and Vauxhall, and the relief of the Northern Line north of Stockwell. If extension beyond Brixton were ever justified they felt that Crystal Palace rather than Croydon would be the objective.

Plans were drawn up, and powers sought in the 1965–66 Parliamentary Session, the Bill receiving Royal Assent on 9th August 1966. In fact, in March 1966 the government had given approval in principle for the scheme, but immediate authority only for preparatory measures, including purchase of tunnel segments. The LT view was that it would be most economical if the tunnelling teams working on the main section of line could be switched to the Brixton extension with the minimum of delay, as it would take some time to re-assemble an experienced team if the existing miners were allowed to disperse (it had proved hard to establish it in the first place). Final Ministerial approval was given on 4th August 1967, and a measure of continuity was achieved. The estimated cost of this extension was £15.9 million.

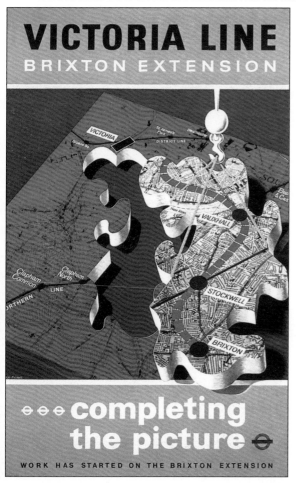

Poster for the Brixton extension. Pimlico station was added later. LT Museum

65

The significance of the authority to begin was not the relative speed of its arrival (though that was welcome), rather the news that the extension might in due course receive an 'infrastructure grant' (government money given for new works and not loaned). For its remaining existence London (Regional) Transport continued to receive similar grants from its masters. The grants were initially made under the Transport Act 1968.

The ground south of Victoria presented a less satisfactory tunnelling medium compared with that on the northern section of line, so rotary tunnelling machines were not used and hand mining with Greathead shields was adopted; the average rate of progress was about 150ft (45m) per week. An unusual hazard existed on the section between Victoria and the River. Several miners reported the existence of a ghost in the southbound tunnel workings, alleged to be near the site where the line passed beneath an old graveyard or plague pit. The 'large black presence' is reported to have induced some consternation at the time.

Vauxhall station site posed major problems. It adjoined the River Thames, close to the outlet of the culverted River Effra, at that point known as Vauxhall Creek; there was therefore much water about, and the clay was overlain by water-bearing gravel. Other complications were the many nearby sewers, and concurrent major road reconstruction, which itself influenced the siting of the ticket hall and access subways. The work was phased, with numerous road diversions made as ticket hall construction progressed. Just below street level the water could be kept out by means of cofferdams, but the ground through which the escalator shaft was to be sunk had initially to be frozen solid (a technique first used at Tottenham Hale).

This view shows work in progress at Vauxhall during 1969. LT Museum

Brixton station awaiting arrival of the Royal Party.
LT Museum

At Stockwell the new platforms would flank those already existing on the Northern Line. Perhaps ironically the Victoria Line works disturbed the access to the wartime deep shelter tunnels, some passages to which had then to be resited. The ground in the area was partially unsound. One Victoria Line tunnel had to be excavated within six feet (1.8m) of the Northern Line; this was very difficult work and at one point a subsidence caused Northern Line services to be interrupted. The existing Northern Line street level station was replaced with a substantially larger joint station on a similar, but enlarged site. The existing pair of escalators was retained and an additional shaft was sunk containing a third escalator and fixed stairway (to save money the provision of escalators was as minimal as it was possible to be).

The site of Brixton station lay on the busy Brixton Road in the town centre and was served by numerous bus routes as well as the nearby British Rail station, although (like Vauxhall) no direct BR interchange was provided (at both stations the main lines were on viaducts and interchange would have been very costly). A twin platform station with two escalators and a fixed stairway was constructed. Beyond the station were twin overrun and siding tunnels, curving to the south and pointing, perhaps a little optimistically, towards Herne Hill to which point they reach nearly half way. To service the extension an additional nine trains (72 cars) were added to the existing rolling stock order and the total number of cars required rose to 316. The extra trains required an additional 5-road car shed at Northumberland Park depot, together with other minor alterations.

The extension took about four years to build and was ready for opening on 23rd July 1971, after trial running from 12th July. The ceremony was performed by H.R.H. Princess Alexandra during the morning, and the public service began at 3pm the same day. The public soon took to the extension, where they found the station finishes and equipment similar to those on the northern section of the railway.

A view of Stockwell station shortly after reconstruction. A second storey was added later.
View of Brixton station shortly after opening. It has recently been modernised. LT Museum

The only additional controlled signalling site was at Brixton where programme machines were provided. Brixton had a scissors crossover north of the station incorporating power-operated 'switch-diamonds' in the central crossing (an idea first used on the Underground on the Central London Railway in 1912); while these successfully gave a smoother, high speed approach to the station they were a maintenance liability and a normal diamond crossing was substituted in August 1983. The southward extension allowed replacement of the scissors crossover north of Victoria station by a trailing crossover (to the later regret of operators). Power to the extension was fed via additional substations at Stockwell and Brixton, the latter at the end of the overrun tunnels.

But this is not quite the end of the story. During the early planning of the Brixton extension the possibility of a station between Victoria and the River was mooted. When powers were sought a route was selected permitting construction of a station in the future if justified. It was not among those authorised in 1967 as the traffic and financial case was at best marginal. However there was strong local support, and the balance was altered when the Crown Estate (a major local landowner) offered easements free for the station site (doubtless substantially increasing the value of their properties). Although the cost was still not wholly justified financially, government approval arrived on 28th June 1968, and Pimlico – the sixteenth station on the Victoria Line – became a reality. Again an infrastructure grant was made.

The works at Pimlico had to take place in waterlogged ground. To deal with the problem the entire area was frozen by means of long pipes through which a refrigerated liquid was passed. LT Museum

Because of its late authorisation Pimlico was not ready when the Brixton extension opened, although it was complete at platform level; trains passed through at reduced speed. The Lord Mayor of Westminster performed the opening ceremony on 14th September 1972, and the station served passengers from 3pm that afternoon. The total cost of the Brixton extension was about £21½ million consisting of a 75 per cent grant from the government and the balance from the Greater London Council (GLC), LT's masters from 1st January 1970.

Pimlico ticket hall shortly after opening. This was the only station on the Victoria Line to open with automatic entry barriers but no exit barriers, reflecting a change of policy since the earlier stations opened. LT Museum

On the subject of ownership it should be noted that for most of its life the Victoria Line had been a part of the London Transport Executive. From 29th June 1984 the organisation passed once more into the hands of central government and was restyled London Regional Transport. Under a provision of the enabling Act a subsidiary company was established on 29th March 1985 called London Underground Limited, and on 1st April 1985 the London Underground system passed into the hands of this new company. With the establishment of a Mayor and Assembly for London a subsidiary body called Transport for London has taken over responsibility for London's Transport, and London Underground Ltd has been transferred to its control from 15th July 2003.

Development and Maturity

So how has the Victoria Line fared since it opened? It is undoubtedly a very busy line and there is no question that it has proved an extremely valuable addition to the London Underground. Not only is it difficult to imagine how Londoners managed without the line for so long, it is also difficult to imagine how financial doubts could have inhibited a start for so many years. Ironically, after accepting the interest-bearing loan from the government, requiring higher fares, London Transport's transfer from central government to the Greater London Council within two years of the line's opening resulted in the whole capital debt being written off. Years of argument thus failed to achieve any particular object, except delay.

A survey of Victoria Line passengers in May 1970 indicated a usage equivalent to 81 million journeys a year already, compared with 58 million a year previously. The 1969 developed estimates for the Victoria Line were between these two numbers (having dropped from the mid-1950s when powers were sought) so traffic was building up most satisfactorily, more so in the central area than at the north end. By 2003 usage had shot up to about 177 million; this sort of increase has put the line under tremendous pressure, far more than it was designed to take, and far exceeds the most optimistic estimate of future usage ever previously made. It was perhaps unfortunate that under government pressure the capacity of the new line (more especially at the stations) had been pared to the bone. It is far more difficult to provide extra capacity on an operating railway than to design it in at the start.

The new line had an effect on traffic on other lines. There was a slight increase at the west end of the Central, Metropolitan and District Lines, but in general traffic levels fell as the new line took off the pressure. In particular there was relief of the eastern and central sections of the Piccadilly Line, the Charing Cross branch of the Northern and the Victoria to Embankment (then Charing Cross) part of the District, though many other areas received smaller relief. This achieved what had originally been intended, though only depressingly briefly. On the Victoria Line itself, by 1970, over three quarters of all journeys started or ended at its six central area stations, and nearly half at either Victoria or Oxford Circus (or both). About half of all journeys were in continuation of another rail journey (by Underground 29 per cent and British Rail 21 per cent), and of the Underground connections half were at one of the four stations with cross platform interchange. Analysis was difficult, but the planners considered that about one trip in five was a newly generated journey while the bulk of trips had switched from some other mode; they thought that about 4000 fewer trips a day were made by car than hitherto, a most useful contribution.

The automatic fare collection system faded away gradually. The plan to introduce it systemwide was thwarted by cost, complexity and a lower level of reliability than had been hoped. In addition the need for enthusiastic support from British Rail (whose tickets appeared on the Underground in huge numbers) was not forthcoming. On the Victoria Line itself the severely limited roll-out of AFC proved burdensome. The huge number of non-encoded tickets presented at Victoria Line stations, which were issued on other lines or by British Rail, meant that no staff savings could be made. The AFC exit gates were only lightly used and thus became a liability; they were removed in 1972 and the attempt to issue AFC style season tickets was abandoned at the same time. Entry gates were retained as these did encourage passengers to buy tickets, although the coding was greatly simplified. During the 1980s a new systemwide ticket system was developed, known as the Underground Ticketing System (or UTS). This required the use of entirely new equipment and new self-contained ticket office suites that superseded all the original Victoria Line ticket offices. A prototype system was installed at Vauxhall on 31st October 1982 to test a range of new equipment. Tickets (now of credit card size) were issued by means of one of two new machines (a 'Tenfare' or an 'Allfare' machine, the former selling the most frequently needed tickets only) that could take money and give change, although manned ticket office windows were retained. The new ticket office suites enabled the booking clerks to service the machines from within the office; the days of freestanding machines were now at an end. A separate note-changing device was also fitted. New-style ticket barriers were also tested, way in and way out, and season tickets were included in the experiment. Judged a success, planning then proceeded for systemwide introduction of UTS that took place from the late 1980s. All ticket offices were rebuilt though at first only stations within Zone 1 (central London) were equipped with the new barriers.

The same-level interchange at Highbury became very much more useful from 1976 when the BR electrification scheme from Hertford North and Welwyn Garden City to Moorgate (authorised in 1971) began operating. The Northern City Line was closed in 1975 for refurbishment to BR standards and a substitute coach service operated. A BR shuttle from Drayton Park to Old Street opened on 16th August 1976, with the full service from Finsbury Park and the BR suburban lines to Moorgate from 8th November. Traffic results on this line have been slightly disappointing, especially off-peak when services have been somewhat cut back (they stop at 8.30pm on weekdays and progressively weekend services have been completely withdrawn). At King's Cross the Midland electrification scheme (in service from July 1983) caused the construction of a new subway from the Piccadilly Line to the Midland City (now Thameslink) station, and a link was also made from the subway to the Victoria Line, which improved railway interchanges and provided a street access from a new building in Pentonville Road.

A serious fire occurred at Oxford Circus on 23rd November 1984; it developed in a passage hoarded off for contractors' use and then spread behind and along the false ceiling of the northbound platform. Although nobody was killed a huge amount of destruction resulted, a number of people were taken to hospital and the Victoria Line service was suspended for over three weeks between Victoria and Warren Street. Temporary finishings were provided on the northbound platform and it was nearly two years before permanent ones were completed, in a style different from other platforms on the line but in keeping with modernisation of the Bakerloo Line platforms (the motifs on the southbound platform were also altered to match). A rather more serious fire occurred at King's Cross on 18th November 1987 when 31 people died; this broke out on the Piccadilly Line escalators and although the Victoria Line was not very much affected the main ticket hall was destroyed. The fire brought about a complete rethink of fire safety matters which eventually resulted in removal of all materials that were either flammable or produced noxious gases in the event of a fire – for example all the melamine ceiling panels on the Victoria Line were replaced by metal ones with a white, inert powder-coated finish. In addition a vast amount of advanced fire safety equipment and updated communications were installed and control room facilities were upgraded.

At Blackhorse Road a theoretical interchange was introduced with BR's Kentish Town–Barking line in 1971 by the mere expedient of showing it on maps; the stations were still physically on different sides of a main road though some desultory through ticketing emerged following pressure. From 14th December 1981 the BR platforms were shifted to a position where a footbridge allowed access to the Victoria Line ticket hall and LUL took responsibility for ticket issuing. This helpful move resulted from a GLC grant of £105,000 in an attempt to improve upon a quite unsatisfactory piece of earlier planning. Tottenham Hale main line station was significantly upgraded in 1992 (with formal opening on 19th March) as it had proved a popular interchange and was a key feature of the new Stansted Express service. Seven Sisters had also proved a popular interchange and the main line station received significant upgrading in 1979 and further improvements (including an escalator to the down platform) in May 1985. LUL improvements were taking place in 2003 and accommodation for trainstaff was being built at ground level in replacement of the less than satisfactory conditions underground.

The remaining stations have stayed largely unchanged since the line opened although there has been piecemeal updating. Finsbury Park station has not changed much at platform level since the Victoria Line arrived, but BR eventually completed a major modernisation of its street level frontage, including the final obliteration of traces of the partly built Northern City Line high-level platforms, which were an eyesore for many years; the scheme was not finally complete until 1984. The Wells Terrace entrance to the station had been rebuilt by LT in the early 1970s and was officially 'opened' on 6th October 1974; this followed construction of a new bus station alongside, significantly improving interchange between buses and the tube and main

The platform tile motifs on the extension south of Victoria: a modern art design for Pimlico (the Tate Gallery), Vauxhall Gardens for the next station, a design suggesting a swan for Stockwell and a 'ton of bricks' for Brixton. Capital Transport

The tile motif at Green Park was replaced in 1979 by a leaf design to match the new Jubilee Line platforms. Capital Transport

line stations, that opened on 21st April 1974. At Green Park new seat motifs were introduced at about the time the Jubilee Line opened in 1979 and a new passageway to the Jubilee Line opened in 1999 as part of the Jubilee extension works. Several other stations have had seat motifs replaced. In general station tiling has been a perennial minor problem in that much of it became loose with the tiles inclined to fall off, leaving unsightly patches, a problem still being addressed today. In some cases major retiling work has had to be undertaken with some stations such as Victoria virtually entirely retiled. Some other features did not prove as successful in real life as had been hoped, thus the original Passenger Information Points soon became redundant though more modern equipment has been installed quite recently, taking advantage of the continuous manning of control rooms.

The 39½ trains of 1967 stock served the Victoria Line well for over twenty years, but by the beginning of the 1980s the automatic driving equipment was acknowledged to be less reliable than prevailing technology and the appearance of the stock was becoming dated. After successful trials it was decided to replace the auto-drive boxes with more modern equipment incorporating a computer and databank that retained (amongst other things) a record of the whole Victoria Line signalling, gradient and station locations. Under normal conditions the new autodrive boxes would accurately pinpoint the train's position on the railway and using the existing track commands would control the train on a continuous basis rather than in response to each discrete command. This was much more accurate and reliable, especially if for some reason a command spot instruction was missed. In the event that the computer system failed or lost its bearings then control reverted to individual command spots that were retained as a backup.

Because of the upsurge of traffic on the Underground during the 1980s, Victoria Line train services had to be increased, creating a shortage of trains. The solution was to import additional cars onto the line using former Northern Line 1972 Mk I stock which was very similar to the 1967 stock. As the Northern Line cars were not equipped with automatic driving apparatus, the motor cars could only operate in the centre positions of Victoria Line trains, requiring a certain amount of remarshalling within the fleet and the creation of an additional 3½ trains, increasing fleet size to 43 trains. Some thirty-one 1972 stock cars were absorbed between 1987 and 1989, allowing also three collision-damaged cars to be replaced.

With other work that it was convenient to undertake at the same time, for example replacing the out of date carrier wave equipment by train radio, the fleet was divided into two types of 4-car unit. The first type, called a single-ended unit, has only one fully-equipped driving cab which has necessarily to operate at the outer end of an 8-car train. The inner cabs, which can be of 1967 or 1972 origin, contained only basic driving equipment for shunting purposes and can only be deployed in the middle of a train where they are not used in service. The other type of unit is called a double-ended unit; in this case both driving cabs are fully equipped. The single ended units are divided equally into those with the fully equipped cabs at either the north or the south ends and an 8-car train can comprise any of four possible combinations of different pairs of units, the only proviso being that there is a fully equipped cab at both ends of the train.

The widespread review of inflammable and potentially toxic materials that followed the serious fire at King's Cross, referred to earlier, also had a big impact on rolling stock. As some of the materials used on trains were now called into question, a wonderful opportunity presented itself to replace somewhat dated interior designs with completely new ones better suited to prevailing conditions. The work took about five years to complete and was undertaken by Tickford Rail at Rosyth Dockyard. In addition to the remodelled interiors, the previously unpainted car bodies were painted

Victoria Line rolling stock – refurbished interior, 1994. Ian Bell

in London Underground's corporate livery that greatly improved the appearance of the trains and made them easier to keep clean. Fully equipped cabs were given the now-familiar red fronts, but emergency cabs (not normally visible) were in the same blue and grey as the rest of the cars.

Prior to refurbishment (during 1989 and 1990) various technical works were undertaken, including the replacement of the air operated passenger alarms by neater electrically actuated units, and the hydraulic parking brakes were replaced by spring-applied parking brakes which applied automatically. Refurbishment allowed the new push-button passenger alarms to be replaced by neater 'pull handle' units that incorporated a two-way intercom so the person using the alarm could speak to the train operator.

On the subject of rolling stock it is worth observing that until around 1986 the periodic heavy overhaul of Underground trains took place at the central overhaul works at Acton. Victoria Line trains reached Acton via Finsbury Park where there is a connection with the Piccadilly Line; each train had to be specially fitted with a tripcock prior to departure from the depot, and on reaching the crossover at Finsbury Park the auto-drive equipment was switched out and the tripcock was cut in instead of the code trip valve. This allowed the train to be driven manually at normal line speed with the tripcock as protection against passing a conventional signal at danger (the process being reversed in the return direction); the stock moves were scheduled during the evening on an 'as required' basis. After 1986 heavy overhaul was transferred to the various major depots and Northumberland Park began to undertake the work for Victoria Line trains, requiring the building of four additional covered sidings.

Stations also bore the brunt of the increase in passengers during the 1980s and 1990s and this immediately highlighted the insufficiency of capacity at a number of additional stations (at Victoria the shortage of capacity was a frequent cause of deliberately restricting entry to the station in the event of the slightest service delay, with temporary closure to inbound traffic during the morning peak ever more frequent). Remedial measures included the fitting in 1996 of an additional escalator instead of a central stairway in the Victoria–District Line interchange flight together with an additional stairway from the Victoria Line to the eastbound District platform. At both Brixton and King's Cross, access to the Victoria Line was via a pair of escalators flanking fixed stairs and at both the fixed stairs were replaced by escalators. In the case of Brixton this resulted in a three-week closure of the station over Christmas 2003 to remove asbestos. Brixton now has a new entrance building also.

In very recent years Tottenham Hale has benefited from a further four-year regeneration project that has transformed at a cost of nearly £6million the upper level of the station and provided a small lift (commissioned in 2001) that offers step-free access from street level (including bus station) to platforms. Various less dramatic improvements have taken place at other stations, such as Vauxhall, in order to keep them reasonably up to date.

King's Cross is the subject of comprehensive redevelopment to meet the needs of the new Channel Tunnel terminal as well as being the focus for major regeneration of the surrounding area; it also needs to handle the much vaunted 'Thameslink' expansion if and when that happens. The scheme overall involves the construction of two new ticket halls and very significant enlargement of the existing 'tube' ticket hall. The new northern ticket hall (that mainly serves St Pancras and the new Channel Tunnel terminal) will also be linked directly to the Piccadilly and Victoria Lines by both escalators and lifts. All ticket halls will also be linked together.

The New Order

During the 1990s, the Conservative government sought to employ private finance to facilitate the delivery of large-scale capital projects that it could not immediately afford. London Underground embraced the opportunity to inject private money into an ageing system and even the Victoria Line, by then itself showing signs of age, was to benefit. Among the projects taken forward this way was the 'Prestige' project to introduce new ticketing technology. This resulted in ticket gates being installed beyond Zone 1 and the introduction of smartcard technology using 'Oyster' smartcards for most tickets other than daily. Other projects benefiting the Victoria Line were enhanced power supplies (including in 2002 the closing of Lots Road and substituting power from the national grid), and a project to enhance telecommunications, named 'Connect'.

The Labour government that came into office in 1997 embraced the private capital concept on an even larger scale and decided to transfer all London Underground infrastructure and rolling stock to three privately owned companies on 30-year contracts; this left London Underground operating staff in the public sector but with privately 'owned' assets and privately managed engineering and maintenance staff. The idea was that the private sector companies would finance the massive investment needed to overhaul the ageing Underground and in turn get their money back over the life of the contracts through performance-related service charges. The essence of the deal was that money could be deployed outside the arcane government funding rules and the risk of things going wrong was borne in theory by the private sector, which was incentivised to make sure that nothing did. A feature of the contracts was that they were based largely on 'output' measures reflecting service delivery, reliability, so-called 'ambience' and general performance; provided that LUL's engineering standards were complied with, the new companies had considerable freedom to decide how the standards were going to be met.

The Victoria Line assets were allocated to the Bakerloo-Central-Victoria Line (BCV) infrastructure company (an LUL subsidiary) in 2000 and after considerable public controversy this company was sold by LUL to Metronet Ltd on 4th April 2003; Metronet is a consortium of W. S. Atkins, Balfour Beatty, Bombardier Transportation, EDF Energy and Thames Water.

Under the new contracts it is a requirement to upgrade the Victoria Line by 31st March 2011, providing a significant increase in line capacity with reduced journey times, more frequent services and improved reliability, together with enhanced passenger comfort and security. Metronet gave some immediate indications of their plans to improve the assets that they now owned, including those on the Victoria Line. Among the promises made was a new fleet of trains, to be built by the consortium's train builder, Bombardier; it was announced that the forty-seven 8-car trains would begin entering service in 2009 with completion in 2012 after an intensive period of delivery stated to be one train every 15 days. Some passenger benefits would come much sooner though. The Victoria Line's life-expired signalling system is to be replaced by a new and more flexible system that will again offer automatic train operation but on headways as close as 90 seconds, allowing significant service improvements. The new signalling is intended to use modern electronics that avoid the need to cut the running rails into insulated sections where the joints are a maintenance liability. The new train protection system is intended to be far more flexible than the existing one which offers only three 'proceed' codes; the new system operates on the (radio operated) 'distance to go' principle which is far less crude and optimises possible headways. The new system has already been ordered from Westinghouse and will use the well-tried 'Westrace' electronic interlockings and a 'Westcad' control centre.

The proposed design for the new trains, due to enter service between 2009 and 2012 following trial use of a prototype train.
Metronet

The slightest unevenness in the train service during the morning peak can result in unacceptable crowding at platform level with passengers having to be held back at ticket hall level, as seen here. This is unfortunately a frequent feature, though most closures are only for a few minutes. Capital Transport

An advantage of the 'Distance-to-go-Radio' (TBS100) technology is that by using trackside radio transmission it is simpler to overlay on existing systems, facilitating the changeover process from one to another. Initially it is planned to overlay the new technology on the existing interlocking machines; by this means, a train operating on either the old or new systems can proceed under the control of the existing signalling and operation in this mode is expected to begin in 2007. When the last of the 1967 stock has been withdrawn the old signalling and interlockings can be withdrawn and all trains will operate purely under the control of the new equipment when the benefits of improved performance can be fully realised.

From the identification in the late 1930s of traffic flows and pinch points that needed attention it took thirty years to complete a remedy – the Victoria Line. Fourteen years were needed to firm up and plan a route, a process hardly helped by a major war. Ten years were needed to argue the case for the money (it being considered marginal), and six years were needed to build the line. Today it carries amongst the highest density of passengers on the Underground and screams for additional capacity. It is an object lesson in planning transport systems in London.

Extensions have been considered but with capacity in the central area so restricted the scope is somewhat limited. The possibility of providing some kind of passenger service on the depot branch, with a passenger station at Northumberland Park, has potential and has been looked at more than once (most recently in 2003 under pressure from the local authority which is keen to regenerate the area). The logistics of doing this means that costs would be high in relation to the benefits gained and the idea would not at present seem to be workable. One thing is certain: if an extension there is to be, it won't be soon.